The Roots of Evil

About the Author and Respondent

NORMAN L. GEISLER

Norman L. Geisler received his B.A. and M.A. from Wheaton College and the Graduate School, his Th.B. from Detroit Bible College, and his Ph.D. from Loyola University. He was an assistant professor of Bible and apologetics at Detroit Bible College from 1959 to 1965 and served as chairman of the Department of Philosophy at Trinity College. He presently serves as Professor of Systematic Theology at Dallas Theological Seminary.

Dr. Geisler's other books include: *Ethics: Alternatives and Issues, Philosophy of Religion, Christian Apologetics, Options in Contemporary Ethics,* and *Miracles and Modern Thought.* He is the coauthor of *A General Introduction to the Bible* and has written numerous articles.

JOHN W. WENHAM

John W. Wenham has an M.A. from Cambridge University and a B.D. from London. He taught in the London College of Divinity and in the University of Bristol. He was vice principal of Tyndale Hall, Bristol, and warden of Latimer House, Oxford.

He is an ordained minister of the Church of England and has served in parishes in Cambridge, Durham, and Oxfordshire. During World War II he was a chaplain in the Royal Air Force and was stationed much of his time in Jerusalem.

He is author of *The Elements of New Testament Greek* and is at work on a series of books relating to the Bible. Published so far are *Christ and the Bible* and *The Goodness of God.*

The Roots
of Evil

Norman L. Geisler

with a response by
John W. Wenham

ZONDERVAN
PUBLISHING HOUSE
GRAND RAPIDS, MI

PROBE MINISTRIES
INTERNATIONAL
DALLAS, TEXAS 75380-1046

Copyright   © 1978 by Probe Ministries International

Library of   Geisler, Norman L.
Congress   The roots of evil.
Cataloging in
Publication Data   (Christian free university curriculum)
                   Bibliography: p.
                   1. Good and evil.   2. Theodicy.   3. Provi-
                   dence
                   and government of God.   I. Title.   II. Series.
                   BJ1401.G44   216   78-9479

ISBN   0-310-35751-9

Place of   *Printed in the United States of America*
Printing

Design   Cover design by Paul Lewis
              Book design by Louise Bauer

85   86   87   88 — 10   9   8   7   6

What Is Probe?

Probe Ministries is a nonprofit corporation organized to provide perspective on the integration of the academic disciplines and historic Christianity. The members and associates of the Probe team are actively engaged in research as well as lecturing and interacting in thousands of university classrooms throughout the United States and Canada on topics and issues vital to the university student.

Christian Free University books should be ordered from Zondervan Publishing House (in the United Kingdom from the Paternoster Press), but further information about Probe's materials and ministries may be obtained by writing to Probe Ministries International, P.O. Box 801046, Dallas, Texas 75380-1046.

Contents

Book Abstract

In this book, various philosophical options are proposed to answer the apparent contradictions between the existence of evil and God. An analysis is made of such systems as illusionism, dualism, finitism, sadism, impossiblism, atheism, and theism. Biblical theism is then evaluated for its ability to answer some of the major questions in the areas of metaphysical, moral, and physical evil.

The Dilemma
of Evil

Chapter Abstract

The basic dilemma of evil is discussed and illustrated in current works of literature.

chapter one

The Dilemma
of Evil

At some time or another, everyone wonders about the existence of evil and suffering in the world. Its presence has touched all, ravaged many, and per- plexed thinking men throughout the ages. Surely, if there were a God in the universe, He would have both the desire and the power to rid the world of evil!

In his book *The Plague,* Albert Camus confronts the reader with this dilemma through the character of Paneloux, the priest of the village. As his community is overwhelmed by the horror of the plague, Paneloux is forced to make a crucial philosophical decision. Either he must have faith that God will bring good out of the evil situation, or he must stand with Dr. Rieux and Tarrou and condemn the evil situation as unbeara- ble and unredeemable. To them, the situation declares either that there is no God, and man is left to struggle in futility, or that if there is a God, He must be the supreme, evil enemy of man. The tension of this per- sonal dilemma is the captivating force in Camus's 11 powerful story.

Not all who have considered the problem of evil have been driven to these two extremes. Some have sought to fit God into the universe by changing the traditional view of His character. They have suggested that if God exists, He might not be all-powerful and therefore not able to rid the world of evil. Others have argued that God is not all-loving but instead is generally unconcerned about the personal tragedy that man faces. This view considers God to be like the professor in Thomas Carlyle's essay *Sartor Resartus*. As the professor looks out upon the masses of people beneath his window and sees them huddled and struggling, he finds himself becoming more and more removed from their problems and tragedies. He is no longer involved with and experiencing their toils and anguish. It is as if he has ceased to be a member of the human race, for now he views their world with compassionless detachment. Similarly, some men think of God as detached and isolated from men, as uninvolved as the professor in Carlyle's essay.

It is not difficult to recall times of tragedy, personal or close at hand. At such times, answers about God and evil seem elusive or unsatisfying. The dilemma is not only intellectual, but also existential. Must one believe that God is cruel, compassionless, impotent, or nonexistent in order to deal with the reality of evil in the world? This is more than an abstract, philosophical question. It touches each and every one of us where we live. And sooner or later, either deliberately or inadvertently, each of us adopts a view with regard to evil.

In this book we will examine some philosophical options that have been proposed to answer the apparent contradictions between evil and a good God. We will look at such systems as illusionism, dualism, finitism, sadism, impossiblism, atheism, and theism. Each will be evaluated for strengths and weaknesses. It is obviously impossible to cover every aspect of these sytems in rigorous detail in this short work; therefore, those who are interested in further detail are encouraged to refer to the list of references under *For Further Reading* at the end of the book.

Philosophical
Options
Concerning Evil

Chapter Abstract

One group of philosophical options seeks to resolve the dilemma of evil by dealing with the basic nature of evil. Illusionism suggests that evil is an illusion; dualism suggests that it is eternal.

chapter two

Philosophical Options Concerning Evil

There are a number of philosophic systems that have been developed to deal with the problem of evil. These can be roughly broken down into two major categories: those that deal with the nature of evil and those that deal with the nature of God. In this chapter we will discuss the options dealing with the nature of evil.

One of these systems, which will be called illusionism, solves the problem of evil by denying its existence. In this system, evil ceases to be a philosophic problem because all of material reality is considered an illusion. Rocks and trees, as well as pain and suffering, are taken to be only illusions. Illusionism thus becomes the basis for a number of religions and philosophies in both the East and the West.

Some Eastern religions, such as certain forms of Hinduism, have a doctrine called monism, which states that all diversity in the world is an illusion.

Is Evil an Illusion?

15

Ultimate reality is both one and good. Therefore, things that appear in this world to be many and evil are actually an illusion. The illusion of the external world is called *maya,* and the illusion of diversity is called *mithya*.

Monists would acknowledge that we may "feel" that such a view of reality is false. Each of us "seems" to experience the world as being diverse and evil, but according to this view, our feelings are false. The famous ninth-century Hindu thinker, Sankara, argued that *Brahman* (Hindu name for God) is the sole reality. The external world only *appears* to be something in the same way a rope appears to be a serpent, until we get closer. Likewise, when we examine the world more closely, we see that the only reality behind the illusion is *Brahman. Brahman* "causes" the world to appear diverse and evil only in the sense that the rope "causes" the serpent to appear.

In the Western world, illusionism has taken a number of different forms. The first proponents of illusionism in the West were the Greek thinkers Parmenides and Zeno. Parmenides (born 515 B.C.) was one of the first philosophers to focus his attention on the area of metaphysics (the nature of real being). He argued that our senses could not be trusted.[1] Parmenides believed that although things may appear to be many and evil, they are in fact, ultimately one and good. Furthermore, he said that a person's senses are easily deceived, and consequently man's present perception of the world as diverse and evil is a false perception.

One of Parmenides' pupils, Zeno (born 490 B.C.), attempted to prove this view through logic. One of his arguments centered around the classic "Race Course Argument" that denied the true existence of motion. A runner starting at point A cannot reach point B, except by transversing a successive number of halves of the distance. In order to travel from A to B, one must travel past the midpoint (M_1). But in order to travel from A to M_1, one must travel past the midpoint (M_2) of *that* distance. And in order to travel past midpoint M_2, one must travel past the midpoint (M_3). Thus in order to travel in any direction, it appears that we must travel across an infinite number of midpoints (M_1 to $M_{infinity}$), which seems to be impossible. If that is true, then, according to Zeno, motion is impossible and therefore just an illusion.

A modern form of illusionism in the West is Christian Science. According to Mary Baker Eddy, "Evil is but an illusion, and it has no real basis." That is, evil is not a real entity, but is instead a false perception; it is the "error of the mortal mind." Christian Science maintains that God is truth and that "there is no pain in truth, and no truth in pain." Sin, sickness, and death, therefore, are mortal illusions that do not exist in reality.[2] Christian Science therefore approaches the problem of evil in exactly the same way as Hinduism and the teaching of Zeno—evil is illusion.

An analysis of illusionism can be summarized by a number of questions that have been posed to followers of this system. First, if evil is an illusion, where did the illusion *originate?* If it is indeed an illusion, why do all experience it from the moment of birth? Does the illusion originate at birth, or is it passed down to each generation?

Second, we might ask, if evil is only an illusion, why does it *seem* to be so real? It was Edward Lear who wrote:

> A certain faith-healer of Deal
> Asserted: "Pain is not real."
> "Then pray tell me why,"
> Came the patient's reply,
> "When I sit on a pin
> And puncture my skin,
> Do I hate what I fancy I feel?"

A third question that should be raised is whether or not there is any *practical difference* between viewing pain or evil as illusion or viewing it as actual reality. Pain or evil is part of the human experience and is encountered by all. Regardless of whether it is viewed as illusory or real, the experience is the same. It could just as easily be said that those who view pain or evil as illusion are actually participating in an illusion themselves: not the illusion or experience *of* pain or evil, but the illusion (or wishful thinking) *that* pain or evil is not real.

In conclusion, it must be noted that although this position is a philosophic option, few consistently hold to it. Those who believe that evil and the world are illusions do not actually function as if this were so. They may maintain that all is an illusion, but if one were to push them in front of an oncoming bus, they would quickly "warm up" to the reality idea!

There is much to suggest that this position of illusionism is less than satisfactory. Both our reason and personal experience appear to deny this view. This leads us to a second philosophical option concerning the nature of evil: dualism.

Is Evil the Eternal Opposite of Good?

Dualism as a philosophical system does not deny the existence of evil (as does illusionism), but instead attempts to explain the presence of both good and evil. It can be found in various kinds of religious thought. Zoroastrianism, a religion based on the teachings of the prophet Zarathustra, was the dominant religion in Persia for more than one thousand years. Followers of this religion pictured the universe as a cosmic struggle of the Good *Ahura-Mazda* against the evil *Angra Mainyu,* who was the chief agent of The Lie. One of the movements within this religion held that both of these agents issued from the first principle (called *Zurvan)* at the beginning of time and have coexisted since.[3]

Perhaps the most classic form of dualism is Manichaeism, the philosophical system developed by the Persian prophet Mani (A.D. 216-276). The chief characteristic of this system is that it rejects any possibility of tracing the origins of good and evil to one and the same source. Evil must exist as a separate and completely independent principle from good. Two primal principles of Light and Darkness have existed coeternally, but independently, each dwelling in its own realm.

We can extract two fundamental arguments from these dualistic positions that hold there are two coeternal, if not coequal, substances locked in conflict.[4] The first argument can be summarized in this way:

> Good and evil are opposites.
> But a thing cannot be the source of its opposite.
> Hence, both good and evil must have existed as eternal opposites.
> Good and evil also are substantial and real.
> Therefore, both good and evil are eternal, but opposite realities.

The first premise in the argument seems obvious enough; evil is opposed to good and vice versa. Likewise, the second seems to follow from the first. How can evil come from good? How can good come from evil? A thing cannot produce its opposite. If this is the case, then both good and evil must have existed independently forever. Since both are equally real, the dualists conclude that there are two eternal but opposite principles and that dualism must be true.

A second argument by dualists is aimed at theism (which denies the eternality of evil) and holds that God is the author of everything. The argument against theism can be formulated as follows:

> According to theism, God is the author of everything.
> But evil is something, i.e., evil is real.
> Therefore, God is the author of evil.

Theists cannot object to the first premise. To do so would capitulate the sovereignty of God. Neither can the theist avoid the second premise, since to deny the reality of evil would be to accept the basic tenet of illusionism. But the theist *cannot* accept the conclusion that God authored or created evil (at least in the direct sense), for that would make God evil. The dualist does not have this theistic dilemma. He simply denies the first premise that God authored everything and portrays evil as a reality outside of God and His sovereign control. Evil is thus eternally there, and God must work the best He can.

Theists have responded to these objections with two points.[5] First, not every opposite has a first principle. Small is the opposite of large, but it does not follow that there is something that has eternally existed as small. Second, evil can be real without being a substance or thing. Evil could be a real privation or lack of some good thing. For example, we acknowledge that blindness is real. We don't refer to it as a real thing. Blindness is the lack of something. It is the *real lack* of sight. Being maimed is a reality. It is the *real lack* of a limb. Nevertheless, a lack of something need not be a substance or thing. Evil exists in a good thing as a lack or imperfection in it, like a hole in a piece of wood. Thus it seems quite possible for evil as lack or imperfection to exist in a system where no evil was ever authored.

Modern Forms of Dualism

Modern philosophical attempts to overcome and synthesize the tensions created by the strong irreconcilability of the dualistic system can be found in contemporary process theology. The proponents of this theology, Alfred North Whitehead and Charles Hartshorne, provide excellent examples of this neoclassical theism.[6] They incorporate God and the world into a bipolar God. One pole of God is the world (God's body), and the other pole is God's mind. God is related to the world as a mind is to the body; God is in the world in the sense that God's body is the world. But since the world is God's actuality (i.e., His body), the view is called pan-*en*-theism (meaning, "all-in-God").

This view holds that the world, with all of its evil, is not really *outside* God. He is directly and intimately related to all there is. Evil is simply the incompatibility of some given factors within the ongoing growth of God. It is this growth that is the "process" of process theology. God is always in the world working for good and harmony. To the degree that we cooperate with God and make available for Him the potential for achievement, there is growth in the "body" of God. Since all moral achievement is stored in God, it is available for future use by others in the ongoing world process.

One of the implications of this view is that God is finite and is in the process of struggling with evil. The final chapter of this struggle, then, has not been written. The outcome is not certain. The triumph of good over evil really depends on man's cooperative interaction with God in this epic struggle. Man's actions, not God's, become the decisive and determining factors. Thus, there is not assured hope. There is no final state of perfection wherein good vanquishes evil. Rather, there is a continual, albeit progressive, and cumulative growth in the amount of achieved value in the universe as realized in the world, with the hope that someday (provided man cooperates) good will triumph. Whitehead calls this growth in value "God's consequent nature."[7]

Critics have been very severe in their comments on contemporary process theology.[8] First, in view of the apparent permanence of natural law and the persistence of evil, they have rightly asked what assurance this process theology can offer. If there is a finite God as proposed, there seems to be no guarantee that the outcome of the battle of good and evil will ultimately end in victory for good. Second, why does this finite God, who cannot overcome evil, bother to engage in such a useless project? If evil is never going to be overthrown and overcome, what is the purpose of His involvement? Certainly, if this is the true view of reality, it is most unsatisfying, especially in the light of man's desire to relieve suffering throughout the human experience.

A third question would be How can such a strange, dualistic combination of opposites as good and evil be absorbed into the nature of God? If that has indeed happened, how can we still consider God good? It would seem that if such a God did exist, then He must be the Devil. We would be forced to relate to a very strange God indeed—one repugnant to most men. Fourth, how could one worship a God so impotent that He cannot even call off the whole process? Isn't this God so paralyzed that He is perilous? Man is called upon to rush to His aid to save Him. Fifth, how could the panentheistic God be considered morally worthy when He allows the sum total of human misery in order to enrich His own nature? Sixth, why does God engage in such a wasteful project in His efforts at self-character building? It would seem to be totally at man's expense.

Seventh, how can a better world be achieved if human activity must bring it about and if so few are aware of their important responsibility? Even if men became aware of the plan and were willing to cooperate, what personal value would it bring to an individual to participate in a process that only *may* bring cumulative value over the next millions of years? A last question that must be asked is how proponents of this theology can avoid making evil illusory when they hold that our victory over evil is really God's vicarious triumph in us. Since we do not experience the triumph of good over evil, how would we know it has even taken place? If the world is mostly illusion, why does it seem so real and why is the illusion so universal? Thus, the problems that plague illusionism discussed earlier also affect this form of dualism expressed in contemporary theology.

In conclusion, it could be stated that although dualism seeks to deal honestly with the reality of evil—rather than avoid it—it is most unsatisfactory. Not only is it a system fraught with problems, but it also fails to provide any sure hope for a better world. Good and evil are locked in an eternal struggle. We are left with the alternatives of leaving good and evil unresolved forever, or with an uncertain, ambiguous hope that it might someday be resolved if we come to God's aid and do our part.

Philosophical
Options
Concerning God

Chapter Abstract

A second group of philosophical options affirms the existence of evil and questions the nature of God. Those offered and analyzed are finitism, sadism, impossiblism, and atheism.

chapter three

Philosophical Options Concerning God

Having discussed the nature of evil, we now turn to a second group of philosophic options that deal with the nature and character of God. If evil is not an illusion and not an eternal entity (as in dualism), then, many reason, there must be something in the character of God that can explain the presence of evil in the world. Three major systems attempt to deal with this dilemma of God and evil without denying the reality of either.

Finitism is a system that holds that God is all-loving but not all-powerful, and therefore He is incapable of destroying evil. *Sadism* holds that God is all-powerful but not all-loving, and thus He is generally unconcerned about destroying evil. *Impossiblism* believes that God is all-powerful and all-loving, but it is either impossible for God to foresee evil, or it is impossible for Him to destroy evil without going contrary to His own will.

A further possibility that will be considered in this chapter is that evil exists and God does not. *Atheism*   25 holds that the presence and reality of evil in the world proves that God does not exist. Instead of making evil an illusion, God is an illusion. Let's first examine the approach of finitism as a solution to the problem of evil.

Finitism affirms that God's power is limited. God exists and He is all-loving, but He is not all-powerful. It is as if He is restricted by heavenly handcuffs and thus unable to destroy evil inthe world. Representatives of this view are such writers as John Stuart Mill, William James, and Edgar Brightman.

On the positive side, we must acknowledge that finitism does give a much more realistic acknowledgement of the existence of evil. Instead of denying its existence (illusionism) or believing that it has always existed (dualism), this approach states that God simply lacks the power to deal adequately with evil. A limited God does not have unlimited power; hence, some forces (in this case evil) may be too powerful for God to handle.

Finitism is therefore an appealing system to many who are involved in social action. This system seems to provide true motivation for human moral achievement within society. To struggle against evil in the world would be to aid God *now* in His struggle against evil. Why struggle against evil if God can and will defeat it without us? This view tells us that He cannot, and therefore our help is vital.

Finitism also appeals to our feelings about God. It tends to provide a much more understandable and relatable God. A finite God can be more easily scaled down to the human understanding. Man is more comfortable in relating to, and cooperating with, a God who really needs him in the struggle against the forces of evil.

However, despite its attractiveness, both theists and nontheists have considered finitism to be unsatisfactory. Nontheists have pointed out a number of serious problems that should be considered.[9] First, why did God create a world in the first place if He knew He could not control the evil in it? Man can perhaps be forgiven for setting out on plans that eventually overwhelm him because of unforeseen circumstances. But what about God? If He did not know what would happen, then we must assume that He is also not all-knowing. If that is the case, are we really talking about a God at all or just a finite creature?

Second, what evidence is there (empirical or historical) to show that good is *really* winning out over evil? All things appear to be continuing on from the beginning of the world with no significant signs of moral advance. If good is winning, certainly our daily newspapers don't show it. Third, how can a finite God assure us of the final triumph of good? With such a God it is equally possible that evil will win out and goodness will be destroyed. If God cannot check the forces of evil, how could man ever hope to do so? Men who work for good may be on the losing side and be destroyed. We are thus led to the same pessimism we encountered during our discussion of process theology. And finally, how can finitism claim superiority as a position because it provides an aid to moral motivation, when other views, such as naturalism, claim the same?

Finitism has also suffered serious attacks from the theists. They ask, how can God be finite when every finite being must be caused? Wouldn't a finite God be no more than a giant creature in need of a Creator to explain its existence? One is reminded of the legendary beings of Mount Olympus who were held to be gods by the Greeks, but were merely amplified humanity. Second, how can a finite God guarantee the overthrow of evil and the final triumph of good? Only an infinite God in sovereign control of the universe can really guarantee the defeat of evil.[10] William James, himself a finite-Godist, unwittingly put his finger on the problem when he said, "The world is all the richer for having a Devil in it, *so long as we keep our foot upon his neck.*"[11] This may be true, but the only guarantee that there is a firm foot on the neck of the devil is an omnipotent God.

Although supporters of finite-Godism claim that

their system encourages social action and resistance to evil, the system can just as easily promote an entirely opposite reaction. For example, a brief review of man's history of resisting evil—an unbroken record of futility, defeat, and misery—might prompt a sense of the uselessness of the whole endeavor. The natural response might be: What's the use? or, Why bother to fight at all?

In conclusion, it must be noted that finitism does not offer satisfactory answers to the question of God and evil. It does not answer why God brought the world into existence if He knew it would be evil. It fails to explain why evil does not appear to be destroyed nor does this view even guarantee that it will. It posits a finite God who is unable to defeat evil or even control the activities of a devil. Therefore, if God is not limited in power, perhaps He is limited in love. This is the philosophical option we will consider next.

Is God All-Loving?

Sadism is the belief that God delights in, or at least is relatively unconcerned about, evil that is inflicted upon His creation. The sadistic God is decidely lacking in love or is even hateful. Sadism is not a widely held position. Most adherents of this position are either bitter theists or satirical atheists.

While some thinkers (including the finite-Godists) have held that an all-loving God is limited in power, the sadistic God is just the reverse: unlimited in power, yet lacking or limited in love. It is not surprising that few thinkers hold this position. The view has little to commend it beyond the bare and bitter fact that, if true, it would at least "explain" the problem of evil. The French philosopher, René Descartes, hypothetically proposed that behind the world there is a malevolent demon who totally deceives men.[12] A number of atheists have attacked the idea of God by using the satire of sadism. It is rare to find a serious person who believes in sadism. Serious sadism leads naturally to atheism.

Nevertheless, it is important to discuss sadism as a theoretical position on evil so that we can determine whether it is possibly true. According to sadism, men suffer evil because God is lacking in goodness toward them. God could deliver us from our woes, but He simply does not care to do so. In fact, some say that God receives a delight from inflicting evil upon us. It is not difficult to see the inadequacies in this sadistic hypothesis.

The first question we might pose relates to our understanding of what is moral. If God is limited in love, He must also be limited in His moral nature. If we are faced with a morally imperfect God, how would we know it? This problem is seen in the inconsistent position of Dr. Rieux in *The Plague*. If we do not allow ultimate reality to be moral, we cannot morally condemn it. In the same way, we would know that God was morally imperfect only *if* there were an ultimate moral standard *beyond* God by which moral imperfection could be measured and found wanting. A theist might argue that by definition the ultimate moral standard beyond this sadistic ''god'' would be the real God. The evil ''god'' would be no more than a finite ''devil.''

Even if we grant the possible existence of a morally imperfect God, there is a second question that should be raised. Charles Hartshorne has observed that the activities of a sadistic God are incompatible with one another.[13] He would have to be both creating and destroying the world at the same time. He would be intimately loving and savagely opposing His creation simultaneously. Human beings would be everywhere faced with the dilemmas of fighting plagues by killing God's creatures (the rats). Such a situation is indeed contradictory.

In summary, it must be stated that although sadism is a philosophic option, it is one that has few proponents. In addition to its inability to provide any base for a significant religious experience, it faces serious philosophical difficulties. If it is unlikely that God lacked the power to deal with evil as we saw in our discussion of finitism, and if it is also unlikely that God lacked the love to rid the world of evil as we have discussed in the foregoing section on sadism, we are left with the alternative that it is *impossible* for God to foresee or deal with evil.

Was It Impossible for God to Foresee or Destroy Evil?

Impossiblism comes in two basic forms. The first form suggests that God did not foresee evil in the world; it attempts to exonerate God from the problem of evil by making foreknowledge of evil intrinsically impossible. The argument might be stated in this way:[14]

> The future can be foreseen only where there is a necessary order of causes and effect.
> But a necessary order of causes and effects is contrary to human free choice.
> Hence, in a world of free creatures it is impossible to foresee evil.

Critics have pointed to a fallacy in the first premise. Does foreseeing demand foreordination (causing it to happen)? Cannot one foresee a head-on collision without causing it? Impossiblism answers this question with a further argument:

> What ever God foresees must come to pass, since God cannot be wrong.
> If God foresees that a muderer will kill his victim, then the murderer must kill his victim.
> But if the murderer must kill his victim, he is not truly free.
> However, free choices demand that he be free to kill or not kill.
> Therefore, it is impossible for God to foresee what the murderer would do, and it is impossible to foresee any evil.

Even to this argument, however, opponents of impossiblism have suggested counter possibilities. If God is an eternal rather than a temporal being, then He does not really *fore*-see anything. Since He is not limited by time (which is a finite dimension), He simply *sees* all things—past, present, and future—in one "eternal now."[15] Therefore, if God does not really *fore*-see, then it may also be true that He does not *fore*-determine free choices.

Following this line of reasoning, a theist may raise a second objection to this form of impossiblism. It is fully possible that an eternal God may simply *observe* in His one eternal now what the murderer is *freely* doing, without *determining* what he does. Free choice does not mean that one *will* do otherwise. It only allows that one *can* do otherwise. God could know what the murderer *will* do without determining that the murderer *must* do it. Freedom, then is not incompatible with God's knowledge of what is yet future to us. If everything is in the present to Him, then He knows with absolute certainty what men will freely choose to do in time.

Another argument against impossiblism is that even if it is granted that God could not foresee evil coming into the world, this in no way would exonerate Him. Surely, it would not be beyond God's knowledge to foreknow that evil *might* occur if He created free creatures. Although He might not know that evil *would* occur, He would certainly know that evil *might* occur in the world. Thus God would still be responsible for making the world, which He very well knew might go evil.

A final problem with impossiblism is that it fails to explain why God continues to allow evil in the world. When He was first surprised with this unfortunate turn of events, why didn't He nip it in the bud? Why has He allowed it to continue unabated? To this second question, a second form of impossiblism offers an answer.

Could God Have Destroyed Evil and Yet Preserved Free Choice?

This second form of impossiblism is more sophisticated than the first. It affirms that it is intrinsically impossible for God to destroy evil without going against His creatures' free choice. The argument can be formed in this way:

> The only way to destroy evil is to destroy free choice.
> But to destroy free choice is itself an evil.

Hence, God would have to do evil to destroy evil. But God cannot do evil; it is contrary to His nature. Hence, God cannot destroy evil.

Despite the seemingly sound argument that this form of impossiblism makes, there are several objections that must be seriously considered. One might argue that in the area of evil "an ounce of prevention is worth a pound of cure." The best way to overcome evil is to prevent it from occurring. Hence, if God had made a world where men were free to do evil but never chose to do so, then evil would never have materialized. In that case, evil would have been a possible option that was never realized. Most people do not choose to do evil even though it is possible for them to do it. Therefore, if it is possible on some occasions to choose not to do evil, why wouldn't it be possible to have a world where people *always* avoided doing evil, even though it was possible that they could choose it?

Certainly this kind of world would be more appealing. If evil doesn't have any purpose, as this view would hold, and if it is simply "a programming error," then why not make evil an option that would never be realized?

By way of analogy, most biblical theists would not picture heaven as a place where all freedom is lost. Yet Christians believe that evil will never occur in heaven. Why not? They believe this, not because there is any indication that men will be restrained from sin against their will, but because men will freely choose not to sin. If it is possible in the Christian heaven to have freedom without evil, why can't we conclude that men could be free and yet avoid all evil in this world? Hence, impossiblism fails to establish its claim that a state of sinlessness is logically incompatible with free choices.

In conclusion, we must realize that if there is a God, it is difficult to imagine that impossiblism is a very likely option. The character of God seems to argue against either form of impossiblism. For the first form of impossiblism, we see that the argument that evil could not be avoided because it could not be foreseen is questionable at best. And even granting that it could not be foreseen, certainly it is reasonable to expect that it could be destroyed or removed by God once it occurred.

The second form of impossiblism is likewise open to question. If God cannot destroy evil without destroying man's free choice, then why couldn't He design a world where evil is a possibility, but doesn't actually occur? If we can conceive of such a world, is it not locgically possible that God in His infinite power could create it?

As we have looked at these three systems, we have seen that each of them has difficulties reconciling the nature of God with the existence of evil. *Finitism* argues that if there is a God, He must not be all-powerful and hence is incapable of destroying evil. *Sadism* holds that if God exists, He must not be all-loving and thus is generally unconcerned about destroying evil. And *impossiblism* argues that if there is a God, it is either impossible for Him to foresee evil or to destroy evil without destroying free choice along with it.

There is another possibility that we should now consider. It is possible to reconcile the nature of God with the existence of evil if we eliminate the possibility that God exists. By eliminating God, we eliminate the conflict.

Does God Exist?

Since evil seems to be real, then perhaps God is not. We experience the reality of evil, but we do not seem to experience the reality of God. Therefore, many atheists have argued that the existence of evil in the world proves that there is not God. Although there are a variety of arguments that have been proposed, the following five examples capture the essence of these philosophical arguments for atheism.

The first example comes from Bertrand Russell, whom atheists the world over have looked to as one of their major spokesmen. Although he did not offer them in just this way, some of his thoughts may be reformulated into a disproof of God.[16]

If there is a God, then He willed moral law.
If He willed it arbitrarily, then He is not essentially good.
If He did not will it arbitrarily, but willed it according to some ultimate standard beyond Himself, then He is not God.
In either case, the traditional God of theism does not exist.

The traditional theist would respond to Russell by pointing out immediately that God's essential *nature* could be moral and hence it could provide the source for moral law. If He did will moral law according to His absolute nature (rather than some ultimate standard beyond Himself), then it would be neither arbitrary nor less than ultimate moral law. Thomas Aquinas argued that moral law is established in this way. Others, like John Duns Scotus (1265-1308), have responded by pointing out that the divine privilege of God to sovereignly will what He chooses includes moral law. The second view, however, leaves open the additional possibility that God may sovereignly alter moral law. Of the two alternatives, the first is probably the strongest to answer Russell's criticisms of God arbitrarily willing moral law. Certainly we are not compelled in view of these difficulties to accept the conclusion that God does not exist.

A second argument that could be considered is similar to our discussion of an all-loving, all-powerful God in the first chapter. It was formualted by Pierre Bayle in the seventeenth century.[17]

An all-powerful God could destroy evil.
An all-loving God would destroy evil.
But evil is not destroyed.
Hence, there is not an all-powerful, all-loving God.

This argument leads either to the conclusion that there is a weak, limited God or a sadistic God in the universe, or that there is no God at all. Since we have considered the first and second possibilities and found them deficient, let us examine the atheistic alternative.

A first objection that might be raised centers around

the ambiguity of the word *destroy* in the argument.

Does it mean to annihilate? If it means to annihilate, we should recall that it would be impossible to destroy evil that has occurred without also doing away with the moral universe and free choice. As was noted earlier, it would be evil to destroy freedom if God has "willed" this to be a moral universe.

If "destroy" however, means to defeat, conquer, or make null and void, then it is possible that this is presently occurring. If the amount of good over evil is greater in the world right now and will be greater still in the future, then good is indeed defeating evil today.

A second objection might point out that the third premise of Bayle's argument has an arbitrary time limit on it. It says in effect that since God has not defeated evil *until now, He never will.* An obvious response to this objection is to recognize that God may *yet* destroy evil in the future. Since the conditions of this destruction can be specified (i.e., through the plan of biblical theism), they can be verified, making this a meaningful position to hold philosophically.[18] Since we are not yet finished with history, it is possible that all evil in history will one day cease.

A third example of an argument that is used to disprove the existence of God deals with the subject of innocent suffering. Although we will discuss this subject in some detail in a later chapter, it is important to address it here as well. There is perhaps no other subject more painful and perplexing than the subject of innocent suffering. We may not be too concerned if a terrorist accidentally blows himself up while trying to place a bomb in a building, but all of us would be deeply moved if a nearby child were killed by the same blast. This kind of suffering seems to argue heavily against the existence of God. The argument can be stated in this way:

> An all-loving, all-powerful God would not allow innocent suffering.
> There is innocent suffering in the world.
> Therefore, there is not an all-loving, all-powerful God.

First, we must note that it is possible, in fact very probable, that suffering of some type will occur in a world where there are morally free agents. People sometimes exercise their freedom in such a way as to bring suffering to themselves or others either directly or indirectly. Many are killed or injured each year due to ignorance, carelessness, neglect, and outright hatred, and it would be impossible for God to act in these situations without interfering with someone's free choice.

Second, we should realize that the real question is not whether the suffering is *innocent* but whether the suffering is somehow ultimately explained and *justified*. We should also note that suffering that has no apparent justification in the present may still be *ultimately* justified. It is possible that all the unexplained suffering in this world will one day be understood and justified. Here again, the limitations of our vantage point in time should lead us to conclude that such an argument against the existence of God is premature and insufficient.

A fourth example of an argument used to deny the existence of God can be taken from the conclusion of the previous discussion. Atheists take this claim that suffering might be ultimately justified and extend the argument to say that:

No unjustified suffering is compatible with God's existence.
There is unjustified suffering in the world.
Therefore, God does not exist.

The responce to this argument is similar to the response to the previous argument. First, it is important to remember that it may be necessary in a free world to allow evil to actually occur. It may be necessary for God to allow innocent suffering in order to give men full moral freedom. If the choice had been ours, we might have made the same decision. And it may be possible that all cases of individual and presently unjustified suffering are justifiable in view of the whole plan in the long run.

Second, it should be noted that the *ultimate* justification for this suffering may be beyond this world. Although we may not be able to see any justification for it, it is possible that the suffering we observe will one day be seen as part of a larger plan for good and thus justified when the entire plan unfolds. If we were to imagine that the entire universe is a philharmonic orchestra in concert, we might designate certain objects as instruments. A series of events or an era of history might then represent a particular movement within the overall concert. The death of an innocent man during this era might be represented by a dissonant chord and the Second World War by several measures of the score. If the symphony had been playing for thousands of years and someone listened to only a few minutes of a very dissonant section, he would not be fair in pronouncing the whole symphony "horrible" or the dissonant part "unjustified." In the same way, it may be that there are some examples of suffering that do not seem justified from our vantage point, but these may nevertheless be ultimately justified.

Third, it should be recognized that evil may have a purpose in this world. Instead of emerging from suffering with bitterness, many people emerge from it with greater maturity. First-order *evils* may be the necessary condition of second-order *good,* both in this world and the next. Few would deny the virtue of patience and mercy, yet patience cannot be produced without tribulation, nor mercy without tragedy.

This last answer, however, seems to lead to a further difficulty, which has been used as an argument against the existence of God. This forms the fifth and last example of an argument used to prove atheism.[19]

> If evil is necessary as a condition for a greater good, then theists cannot work against evil without working against the greater good God ordained.
> But it is right to work against evil and suffering in the world.
> Hence, theism is wrong, and there is no God.

In this argument, the atheist is using against the theist a form of Camus's dilemma presented in *The Plague.*

The first response to this position might be to point out that, strictly speaking, this is not really an argument against God. For example, it would be *possible* for there to be a God who does not wish His followers to work against suffering.

A second, and more important, response would be to examine the premise that theists cannot work against evil without working against God. There are two major concerns that should be explored. First, this premise confuses the *permission* of evil with the *promotion* of evil. The theistic position is that God has *permitted* evil to occur, but this does not mean that God (or man) must *promote* evil. To protect their child from the pain of falling down, parents could keep a toddler in high-chairs and strollers. However, loving parents allow their child the pain of scraped knees and elbows so that he may gain the greater good of learning to walk. They are permitting the evil of cuts, bruises, and tears so that the child may achieve the benefits of walking, and later of riding a bicycle. This is, of course, something quite other than promoting evil as in a case of child abuse.

A second major concern with the premise that theists cannot work against evil without working against God is that biblical theism rejects such a notion. The biblical theist is, in fact, admonished not to *promote* evil but to *promote* good in the world and relieve the suffering in the world (Luke 10:30-37).

In each of these arguments, as well as in many others that have been devised to show that there is no God, there is a built-in boomerang. As C. S. Lewis pointedly observed, one must *imply* God in order to *deny* God.[20] To complain about unjustified evil in the world, one must also suppose an ultimate standard of justice beyond the world. In other words, if there is no absolute standard (i.e., a God who is or has an absolute moral standard), then in order to complain about unjustified evil in the world, one must "smuggle in" the concept of an absolute (such as is provided by theism) and assume that there is an ultimate, absolute standard of justice beyond this world. To impune God's behavior based upon one's own culturally or historically derived ethic is self-defeating. If, in fact, God is there,

then His ethic would naturally supersede all culturally
derived ethics of men. It is absurd on the surface to
censure an ultimate and infinite God on the basis of
one's relative ethic; to do so is to take the place of God
for oneself. The only possibility left for condemning
Him would be to accept His revealed standard of justice and then maintain that He failed to live up to it.

This ultimate standard is precisely what the theist
means by "God." God is the ultimate standard of good
beyond this world. The atheist's argument is self-
destructive. In his attempt to press the case and disprove God by the existence of evil, the atheist must
imply what he wishes to *deny*. He must either argue *for*
the existence of God or lose his basis for argument.
The ultimate standard of good cannot be evil any more
than a yardstick can be less than three feet. In order to
prove that "God" is evil, one only shows that he has
demoted God #1 (who is supposed to be good) to a
"demon" (who does not care about evil in the world)
by appealing to God #2 as an ultimate standard of
good beyond which there is no appeal.

If we return to the case presented by Pierre Bayle,
we can see this difficulty. His argument was that if
there were an all-loving, all-powerful God, He would
destroy evil. But since evil has not been destroyed,
God must not exist. The boomerang of the atheist's
argument can be seen in the following answer to
Bayle's argument:[21]

> An all-powerful God *can* defeat evil without de-
> stroying free choice.*
> An all-loving God *will* defeat evil without destroy-
> ing free choice.
> Evil is not yet fully defeated.
> Therefore, God will fully defeat evil in the future.

Notice that according to this argument, it is only an
all-loving and all-powerful God who can guarantee
that evil will ultimately be defeated. The fact that evil

---

*If good and evil men are finally separated according to their free
choices, and if good thereby permanently triumphs over evil, then
evil will have been defeated without destroying free choice.

is not yet defeated does not automatically eliminate God. On the contrary, it may be that evil will yet be destroyed, and it will take an all-powerful, all-loving God to effect this. Indeed, if there is such a God, the argument declares that evil *will* be destroyed, since He has the omnipotent power to assure the accomplishment of the task. In the same manner, injustices in this world do not call for the elimination of God, but rather call out for His intervention.

In conclusion, we have seen that there are a number of philosophical options that deal with the nature of God in attempting to explain the existence of evil in this world. *Finitism* deals with the question of whether God is all-powerful. *Sadism* questions whether God is all-loving. *Impossiblism* asks whether it is possible for God to foresee evil or whether it is possible for Him to destroy evil without destroying free choice. And finally, *atheism* questions whether God exists at all.

In the next chapters, we will look at the last possibility: that God does exist with these characteristics of being all-loving, all-powerful, and that evil, though real, is not eternal. This system of *theism* will be analyzed to see if it can answer the basic problems in the areas of metaphysical, moral, and physical evil.

The Theistic Explanation of Evil

Chapter Abstract

Two types of theistic options are proposed, and biblical theism is selected and applied to the metaphysical and moral problems of evil.

chapter four

The Theistic Explanation of Evil

As we begin our discussion of theism, it will be very helpful to distinguish between two different kinds of theistic solutions to the problem of evil. These can be classified into two different systems of natural theology called theodicies.* The first is attributed to the German philosopher Gottfried Wilhelm von Leibniz (1646-1716). It will be called "the greatest world" theodicy. The second form is implied in various theistic works from Thomas Aquinas to the present and will be labelled "the greatest way" theodicy.

According to the greatest-world theodicy, this present world is "the best of all possible worlds." There are many elements of the theodicy of St. Augustine (354-430) that accord with this view. He saw evil as a necessary ingredient in life just as an ugly piece in a mosaic is part of the total beauty of a whole work of

---

*Theodicy means literally "God's justice." It is a term that means a rational defense of the justice of God in view of the presence of evil in the world.

art.[22] Likewise, strikingly beautiful highlights in a work of art are striking precisely because surrounding background areas are painted to recede. According to St. Augustine, even adultery, rooster fights, and the very flames of hell are all part of an overall portrayal of good.[23]

Leibniz amplified and popularized this thesis in his now famous "this is the best of all possible worlds" view. Other worlds were logically possible, but this world was morally necessitated by the nature of God. The reasoning behind this view goes like this:

> God is the best of all possible beings.
> The best of all possible beings cannot do less than His best, since it is evil for God to do less than His best.
> God's nature as best demands that He make the best possible world (if He wills to make one).
> This world is the world that God made.
> Therefore, this is the best of all possible worlds.[24]

In this argument, it is difficult to determine the precise meaning of the words "this world." It may mean "this present world," "the world at any stage of its development," or "the whole course of world history." For the sake of philosophical clarity (not necessarily historical accuracy), we will take the words "this world" to refer broadly to a part or the whole of human history.

If this is what is meant by "this is the best of all possible worlds," then surely Voltaire was right in his classic satire *Candide*. One does not have to be the misfortunate Candide in order to conceive of numerous ways in which this world could be improved. One less rape, one less war, one less cancer victim would have improved the world at any stage. But if the world is actually improvable, then it is not the best. In fact, it could be easily said that if this world is the "best possible," then the best is downright rotten! This system simply redefines evil as good.

The theist, however, need not be caught in the best-world theodicy. He need not either pronounce evil as good or attempt to justify the evils of this world in view of some alleged overall good they help portray. There is certainly a more viable and satisfying alternative.

The second approach, the greatest-way theodicy, does not claim that this is the best of all possible worlds. On the contrary, it admits that the world *is* evil and is perhaps nearer to being the worst possible world than the best. However, this view also holds that this evil world is the best possible *way* to the best world.

Perhaps there is no better way for an all-loving, all-powerful God to defeat evil and produce a greater good than for Him to permit this present evil world. For example, there is no way to produce a great football player without the preconditioning of painful practice. So also, there is no better way to have good muscle tone than to endure the painful experience of physical exercise. Evil may be a precondition for greater good. (This is often true presently and individually. It may also be true ultimately and collectively.) In the following chapters, we will propose this and elaborate on it as the most tenable approach to the problem of evil in the world.

The Metaphysical Problem of Evil

The best way to describe and analyze the greatest-way theodicy is to apply it to the metaphysical, moral, and physical dimensions of the problem of evil. Let's look first at the metaphysical problem of evil. The question can be posed in the following way:

God is the author of everything in the world.
Evil is something in the world.
Therefore, God is the author of evil.

Most theists are unwilling to accept the conclusion that God is in any meaningful way the direct ''author'' of evil.[25] To theists, the absolute source of all good cannot also be the fountainhead of evil. Furthermore, since God is good, He cannot do evil. Therefore, it is to the second premise that most theists take objection. There have been three major responses to this second premise.

Augustine had personally struggled long with this problem, and it is not surprising that he wrote more about it than any other theists. A summary of his position is as follows:

**Evil Is
a Privation
of Good**

God is the author of everything in the created universe.

Evil is not a thing or substance; it is a privation or lack in things.

Therefore, it does not follow that God created evil.

By privation, Augustine means a lack of something or an absence of something that should be there. Sickness can be considered a privation (lack) of good health. Evil could be the lack of good.

Augustine advanced two arguments in favor of this view that evil is not a substance. First, God is good and the author of all good. Hence, whatever He created is good like Himself. Nothing can be the source of its opposite. But God is good and is the creator of everything. It follows, then, that everything God made is good and that there are no evil *things*. The evil that exists does not exist in and of itself but only as a corruption or privation of good things, which were made by God.[26]

Augustine's second argument goes like this:

When what we call evil is not present in a thing, then the thing is better.

But when all of what we call good is taken away, then there is nothing left at all.

Therefore, Augustine concludes that "if after the evil is removed, the nature remains in a purer state, and does not remain at all when good is taken away, it must be good which makes the nature of the thing what it is, while the evil is not nature, but contrary to nature." Hence, "no nature as far as it is a nature is evil; but to each nature there is no evil except to be diminished in respect to good."[27] A man born without sight is subject to an evil. The evil is the lack or privation of sight— something that belongs to the natural order. Evil does not exists in itself but only in another as a corruption of it. Evil is therefore an ontological* parasite!

To say that evil is a privation is *not* the same as saying that it is a mere absence or negation of good. The power of sight is found neither in a blind man nor in a rock. But it is a privation for the blind man, whereas it is a mere absence in the rock. A privation is the absence (or lack) of something that ought to be there.

**Evil Is Not
a Mere Absence
of Good**

As well, metaphysical evil is not a mere negation or unreality. Privations are real and physical. Blindness is a real and physical lack of sight. Being maimed is a positive and real lack of a limb. Sickness is a real physical lack of good health. A rusty car, a moth-eaten garment, and a wounded body are physical examples of real corruptions in otherwise good things. In each case, there is a real lack or corruption that leaves what remains in a state of incapacitation.

If God is the creator of everything that exists and if everything He made was good, then where did the privations in the natures come from? What or who caused the corruption of their natures? Augustine's answer to this question is twofold.

**God Is Not
the Author of
the Privation**

First, God is the supreme and incorruptible good. Augustine stated, "For the chief good is that than which there is nothing better, and for such a nature to be hurt is impossible."[28] As the source and standard of all perfection, God cannot be less than absolutely perfect. God is simple perfection, and an absolutely simple being cannot be destroyed. Since God is infinite and without composition, He cannot be torn apart or decomposed. But with creatures, this is not so. Every created thing is composed and is therefore by nature decomposable. For Augustine, anything *of* God is God, and there is only one. All other things are *from* God but not *of* God. "For *from* Him are heaven and earth, because He made them; but not *of* Him because

---

*Ontology is the branch of metaphysics dealing with the nature of being, reality, or ultimate substance.

they are not of His substance.''[29] So creation is not *ex Deo* (out of God), it is *ex nihilo* (out of nothing). It is for this reason that created beings carry within their very nature the possibility (but not necessity) of nonexistence. Creation makes evil possible, since anything that is created can be destroyed or deprived. But the very nature of God is such that He *cannot* be the author of creaturely corruption.

The second answer of Augustine to the question of what or who caused the privation in the good things God made is found in free choice. Certainly God as the absolutely perfect One could not be the cause of evil. ''For how can He who is the cause of the being of things be at the same time the cause of their not being—that is, of their falling off from essence and tending to non-existence?'' What then is the metaphysical cause of evil? There is none. Metaphysical evil is no thing and therefore needs no cause. As the songwriter said, ''Nothing comes from nothing; nothing ever could.'' Nothing cannot cause something, and the only something there is to create anything is God, but God cannot cause the corruption in the nature of these created things. ''For as far as they are corruptible, God did not make them; for, corruption cannot come from Him who alone is incorruptible.''[30]

If there is no metaphysical cause for the corruption of being, then how did evil arise? For Augustine, the ultimate solution to the metaphysical problem is moral. Free choice is the cause of the corruption of the good world that God made. One of the good things an absolutely good God made was the power of free choice. It is good to be free, but with that freedom comes the capability of actualizing evil. Since man is finite, he is capable of evil. His free choice changes metaphysical evil from being a theoretical possibility to an actual reality. Augustine wrote, ''Sin is indeed nowhere but in the will'' and ''justice holds guilty those sinning by evil will alone. . . .'' If we asked Augustine what caused the choice of evil, he would reply, ''What cause of willing can there be which is prior to willing. . . ? Either will is itself the first cause of sin, or the first cause [i.e., a free creature] is without sin."[31] Or to restate it, free choice is the first cause of evil. It is meaningless to ask what caused the *first* cause (free choice) to choose evil. If free choice is the first cause, then there is no going beyond the first cause for an explanation. The *fact* of free choice is good, but the *act* of choosing evil is bad. So the question of why evil arose is answered only by the fact that free creatures chose to do evil. It is meaningless to ask for any prior reason.

It is meaningful, however, to ask *how* evil arose. For Augustine, evil is the corruption that arises when a good but potentially corruptible creature turns away from the infinite good of the Creator to the lesser good of the creatures. "For evil is to use amiss that which is good." Free choice is good, but the misdirection of free choice is evil. Evil "is not the striving after evil nature but the desertion of better [nature]." Evil occurs when "the mind being immediately conscious of itself, takes pleasure in itself to the extent of perversely imitating God, wanting to enjoy its own power [and], the greater it wants to be the less it becomes. Pride is the beginning of all sin. . . ."[32] While evil is not metaphysically caused, we must conclude that metaphysical evil comes about when moral pride occurs; when the creature considers its own finite good more important than the creator. Pride is the ultimate source of privation.

It is now important that we leave our discussion of the metaphysical problems of evil and consider the theistic answer to the moral problem of evil. As we saw in the previous chapter, finitude makes evil possible and in the present chapter we see that free choice has led to the reality of evil. Our question might now be, Why did an absolutely good God make creatures with free choice when He knew they would choose evil? There seem to be some serious objections that could be raised about this free-choice explanation for moral evil within the theistic framework.

The Moral Problem of Evil

We tend to be impatient with our political leaders when they don't produce. It's quite natural, then, to expect someone with the resources God has to supply mankind with perfection now. This is, in fact, what makes the problem so acute for traditional theism with its insistence on an absolutely perfect, all-knowing, and all-powerful God. A lack in any one of these areas (a God that is not all-knowing or all-powerful would be an "out" for the Christian theists. For instance, if God were not all-knowing, then He might be exonerated for not foreseeing that evil might occur. But impossiblism has already been discussed and rejected. Likewise, if God were limited in love and/or power, one could understand why He allows evil to continue. But both sadism and finitism are likewise inadequate and incompatible with theism. There is one of two possible alternatives. The view, which we will call necessitarianism, suggests that God was forced to or needed to create.

Necessitarianism is usually associated with pantheism. For pantheists creation flows necessarily from the very nature of God. Plotinus (205-270), the founder of Neoplatonism, felt that creation was as necessarily connected to God as rays are to the sun. "Try all you will," he said, "to separate the light from the sun or the sun from the light, forever the light is the sun."[33] Likewise, Benedict Spinoza (1632-1677) held that "from the necessity of the divine nature must follow an infinite number of things in infinite ways."[34] Thus, theists have sometimes unwittingly brought in pantheistic solutions to the question as to why God created.[35] This kind of reasoning is both unfortunate and unnecessary. The answer to why God created is the same as to why man sinned: free will. God freely chose to do so.

The cause of creation is God's free choice. This is not indeterminacy but self-determination.* No external necessity can be laid upon an absolutely perfect and necessary being. If God is the absolute sovereign power in the universe, then nothing or no one can dictate anything to Him. The only thing the theistic

---

*Free choice means self-caused actions. No action is uncaused, and actions caused by another are determined (i.e., not free). Hence, free actions are self-caused.

God *must* do is to will His own absolute goodness.
Everything else he may or may not do. More precisely,
the theistic God need not *do* anything. He simply must
be God. For the theist the *cause* of creation is free
choice and to ask what caused the first cause to do this
is meaningless. It is, nevertheless, meaningful to ask
for the *purpose* of creation. But even here, theists
sometimes borrow from pantheists.

The theistic God did not create because He *needed*
to do so for His own self-fulfillment or for other alleged
needs. An absolutely perfect being does not *need* anything. Likewise the God of biblical theism did not
create because He was lonely and needed fellowship.
The interpersonal fellowship in the tri-unity of the God
of the Bible is presented as absolutely perfect. The
Trinity is an eternal and essential community of person
in perfect and intimate fellowship. Why then (i.e., for
what purpose) did God create? A more consistent theistic answer would be: because He wanted (i.e., willed)
to do so. It is sufficient to answer that God is love and
like a loving father, He wanted a family with which to
share His love. God does not *need* love, but if He *is*
love, it is understandable that He would *want* to love
and to be loved. Many theists also believe that God
created so that He could be worshiped and enjoyed by
man forever for who He is. This surely is not incompatible with His desire to give and to receive love.

Whatever the case, necessitarianism is not a viable
solution for theism because it is based on some lack in
God and His nature. The God of biblical and traditional
theism was free not to create at all. But herein lies the
severest test of theism on the problem of moral evil.
God freely chose to create a world He knew would turn
against Him and would bring upon itself and others
untold human misery and woe. Why? Of all the alternatives open to a theistic God, it would seem that He
chose the worst possible choice of at least four alternatives. These are: (1) The theistic God could have chosen not to create any world at all, (2) He could have
chosen to make a world without free creatures in it, (3)
He could have brought about a world where creatures
were free but would never sin, (4) He could have

created a world where men are free and do sin. These four possibilities can be called: No World, Amoral World, Morally Innocent World, and Morally Fallen World. Now of these four possibilities, it seems that God chose the only one where evil would occur, and this seems to be a blatant contradiction to His nature as described by theists.

In view of this situation, the burden resting upon the theists is to show that no other alternative creation plan that God could have carried out would have been morally better than permitting this Morally Fallen World. There is an underlying assumption to this argument implied by the nontheist and accepted by many theists that will be adopted in this discussion. It is this: the theistic God must do His moral best in whatever He chooses to do in the moral way. To do less than His best would be an evil for God, as it is for man. We know what we would think of a person who would help rescue only one person and then sit and watch three others drown. Likewise, a God who could have done better but did not, would thereby be less than the absolutely perfect Being theism claims Him to be. In the next chapters, we will examine some of these other possible worlds and determine whether they provide a more satisfying alternative than the Morally Fallen World we now inhabit.

Moral Options:
The Worlds That
Might Have Been

Chapter Abstract

Various types of possible worlds are proposed as better moral candidates than the present world we inhabit and these possible worlds are evaluated.

ı

chapter five

Moral Options: The Worlds That Might Have Been

In the Gospel of Mark, Jesus said it would have been better if Judas had never been born (Mark 14:21). Would it not, likewise, have been better if this sinful world had never come into existence? Wouldn't it be better not to have any world than to have this evil world? Why didn't God write off the whole idea of creating a world?

Initially we must note that it is meaningless to try to make a moral judgment where no moral comparison is possible. In order to make a comparison, there must be something that two or more things have in common. There is no common element between nothing and something. The objection reduces to this statement: "It would have been *better morally* for God to have chosen a nonmoral alternative." A nonworld has no moral status, nor metaphysical status. We are not even comparing apples and oranges, since both are fruit and

Why Didn't God Choose Not to Create?

55

can be compared as such. However, no world and a morally bad world have nothing in common.

Further, to make a moral comparison only between no world and a morally evil one is to miss the actual claim of this theistic theodicy. The only claim that is made for this position is that the present world is only the *best way* to a morally better world. The real comparison should have been between no world and the best of all possible worlds that will *result* from this present world. If that comparison is applied, then we are actually back to our central question as to whether God chose the best of all possible ways to the best possible world.

The statement by Jesus about Judas does not apply to this point for several reasons. First, we are not talking about a world where all are lost (like Judas) but one where many are saved (where the greater good is achieved). One might rightly question a world where all are lost compared to one in which some or all are saved. Happily, biblical theism knows no such world where all are lost. Second, the statement of Jesus about Judas was meant to be a moral comparison; it was not a comparison of the merits between nonbeing and bad existence. It was probably a hyperbole indicating the severity of Judas's sin. Elsewhere such statements are made to describe the severity of the sin that was in question. In one instance, Jesus simply called Judas's act a "greater sin" than other sinful acts (John 19:11). In parallel thoughts, Jesus used the same type of hyperbole to indicate severe judgment by using the phrases "it would have been better if" and "more tolerable for" (Luke 17:2; 10:14). Thus, it is safe to say that this statement was not intended to imply that no world is better than the present world. No world is not better morally than the present world, since a nonworld has no moral status.

Why Didn't God Create an Amoral World?

Another possibility might be to create a world of animals, or better, a world of robots who cannot do evil and are free of the moral blemishes we find in man.

The response to this suggestion is similar to the previous example. There is no moral comparison that can be made between a moral world and an amoral world. It is not meaningful to say that an animal world is *morally* better than a human world because an animal world is, in a moral sense, nongood or not-good (i.e., the absence of morals), whereas this human world is morally *bad* (the presence of morals). But there is a vast difference (actually no comparison at all) between nongood and bad. A cow is nongood in a moral sense, but it is not morally bad. Of course it would be better to have a world that was both metaphysically and morally perfect, but if moral perfection is possible (via free choice), then metaphysical imperfection will also be possible. Creatures are finite and corruptible. There is no way to say a world of nonmoral creatures would have been morally better. In fact, the question is not even a moral question.

As was argued earlier, freedom without sin is not logically impossible. Jesus was free to sin and did not. Men are free to sin and often do not. Therefore it is logically possible that they could avoid sin on other occasions, too. Further, biblical theism asserts that heaven will contain free people who will *never sin*. Why then did God not create a world where all men were free but where they simply would never choose to exercise their free choice to do evil?

There are several responses to these questions. First, it is possible that no such world would ever have materialized. Not everything that is logically possible actually happens. My nonexistence is logically possible, but is not *actually* the case, since I do exist. It is logically possible that the United States could have lost the Revolutionary War since other armies have lost against lesser odds. But they won, and it is futile to speculate what might have been or would have been, if they had lost. Likewise it is logically possible that no one would ever sin, but the fact is that men have *actually* sinned. In short, we contend that in a world of free choice a state where no one ever sins is logically possible, but it is in the nature of freedom that God could not secure such a state. Nothing He could build into a free world would make sinlessness inevitable.

Second, it may not be possible without tampering with human freedom, to produce a free world where men never choose to sin. If a man decides to sit on the back porch but is chased by hornets to the front porch, did he freely choose to go? Not really. He was coerced by physical threat against his real choice. And in this sense, it would be less than perfectly loving for God to coerce someone against his real choice. Love is persuasive but not coercive. Forced love is not really love at all. The refrain from a popular song said, "You don't know how many times I've wished that I could *mold* you into someone who would cherish me as much as I cherish you." Why didn't God create creatures that would love Him and do only good as much as He supposedly loves us and does only good?

It may be that God could create a world where all men would always choose the good by programming them (like behavior conditioning) so they would never *want* to do evil. But it must be noted that such programming on man would truly go "beyond freedom and dignity." And this itself would be a violation of the freedom of men and just cannot be in a moral world. Freedom is an absolute essential to a truly moral universe. Love cannot be programmed. Love is personal and subjective, and no amount of impersonal and objective programming can automatically and inevitably produce a loving response. Some divorces will occur no matter how loving and desirous one partner is of reconciliation.

Third, a world where evil never occurred is morally inferior because it would never provide occasion for achievement of the highest virtues or the highest degree of other goods. The highest goods are dependent on the preconditioning of evils. Where there is no tribulation, patience cannot be produced. Courage is possible only where fear of evil is a reality. If God created a world where evil never occurred, He couldn't produce the greatest good.

Lest this seem too harsh, the reader must remember that often even that which we see as evil may in fact be good, for it brings us to our goal of the best of all possible worlds. C. S. Lewis gives this illustration of a person walking a dog:

> If the animal gets his lead wrapped around a post and tries to continue running forward, he will only tighten the lead the more. Both dog and owner are after the same end, forward motion, but the owner must resist the dog by pulling him opposite. The master, sharing the same intention but understanding better than the dog where he wants really to go, takes an action precisely opposite to that of the dog's will.[36]

In a similar way, free will allows us to wrap around a post in this world. We experience harm or evil, which we interpret as a setback. Yet such "setbacks" can not only be the way to the best of all possible worlds, but they can also provide a context by which the highest virtues can be realized.

But we might also ask, how can evil be allowed in cases where there are those who do not respond positively? Pain and evil make some people better people, but they also make others bitter. In response, we might point out that it is a greater good to at least have the opportunity to achieve the highest virtues and pleasures even though those virtues are not always attained by everyone. As Peter Koestenbaum has observed with splendid insight, this world is not the best possible world for man but "the world as he finds it offers him the maximum possible opportunities . . . for ultimate satisfaction."[37] An evil world offers opportunities for the experience and expression of goodness and love not possible without the presence of evil.

In conclusion, a hypothetical world where sin never occurs may be logically possible but it may be actually unachievable and is morally less desirable. A world without sin is not the best of all possible worlds. The best possible moral world is where men are fully free and yet where the higher goods are achievable and a final cure is realized. This fallen world is not the best possible world, *but* it is the best *way* to obtain the best possible world. And by the "best possible world" we don't mean the best world conceivable but the best world *achievable* with fully free creatures.

Some theists have argued that God's love will never let men go until He wins them over to His side.[38] There are two fatal flaws in this view from the standpoint of biblical theism. First, it is not in accord with the teaching of the New Testament. The New Testament does speak of a time when men will be separated like sheep from goats and it does tell us that there will be those who will be cast into hell. Certainly the doctrine of hell is not pleasant, but it would be dishonest to say that the New Testament does not teach that some men will go there forever. It certainly cannot be argued that belief in hell is an illusion, for even nontheists, like Walter Kauffmann, have admitted that "it neither follows that everybody who believes in hell is prompted by wishful thinking nor does it follow that the belief originated in this way."[39] The biblical theist believes in hell and not without some good justification, as the next point will indicate.

Second, theists who argue that all men will eventually be saved do so on what seems to be a misunderstanding of divine love. Love is not coercive. Love allows the loved to respond freely. If the loved does not want to be loved, divine love does not force itself upon the one loved. As C. S. Lewis aptly put it, "There are only two kinds of people in the end: those who say to God, 'Thy will be done,' and those to whom God says, in the end, *'Thy* will be done.' All that are in hell, chose it."[40]

The mistake in the soul-making theodicy is to assume that God will change man at any and all costs. Love does not *make* souls but instead allows others to choose for themselves. A gigantic soul-making theodicy would not be a theodicy of love. It looks, rather, like a cosmic behavioristic modification that goes "beyond freedom and dignity." If it costs man's free choice (which is essential to his humanness), then the cost is too high. Without freedom to decide for oneself, there is not true and mature humanity. As an Old

Testament prophet put it, there comes a time when God must say, "Ephraim is joined to idols, let him alone" (Hosea 4:17). God will not continue to disturb men with manifestations of a love they do not desire. As Lewis states elsewhere, "The only place outside heaven where you can be perfectly safe from all the dangers and perturbations of love is hell."[41]

Theism would be better advised to stick with the biblical concept of a God so loving that He granted His creatures the ability to say no to divine overtures of love. This is a *soul-deciding* theodicy, and it seems more congruent with perfect love. What frustrates good men is evil, and what frustrates evil men is good. Heaven is a place where there will be no more evil to frustrate good men, and hell is the place where there will be no more good to frustrate evil men. God is simply saying to each, "Be it as you wish, forever." Heaven and hell, then, are merely a permanentizing of what men freely will. As the French atheist Jean Paul Sartre correctly observed in his play *No Exit,* the door of hell is locked on the inside by man's free choice. Man is condemned to his own freedom.

Why Not a World Where All Will Be Saved?

Some antitheists have argued that God could have created a world where everyone would eventually be saved. In a world where everyone would be saved (universalism), permitting evil is justified by the long-range result of universal salvation. But the biblical theist claims that God created a world that He knew would contain many people who would go to an eternal hell. Why? In reply, the biblical theist points out that "the Lord is patient . . . , not wanting anyone to perish" (2 Peter 3:9). However, God will not force them to be saved against their will. God is love, and forced love is not love. Forced love is rape, and God is not a divine rapist! God, too, longs for all men to be saved, but not against their will. Jesus said, "O Jerusalem, Jerusalem . . . how often I have longed to gather your children together, as a hen gathers her chicks under her wings, but *you were not willing*" (Matt. 23:37). God does not want anyone to perish, but

He wants "everyone to come to *repentance*" (2 Peter 3:9). God will not save men *at all cost*. He is not a Master manipulator who will twist the wills of people into conformity. God is not a puppet-maker but a soul-lover.

But why, it may still be asked, did God create a world where He knew that not all would be saved in the end? If it is logically possible to have a world where all will be saved eventually, then why did not God create such a world? The answer is simply that God would have if He could have. But not everything logically possible is *actually achievable* with free creatures. Why won't some young women marry some young men who propose to them? The answer is simply because they do not will to do so. Likewise, some creatures do not will to love God. In no world that God could create would *all* men freely choose to love God. The Christian is assured by Scripture that God will produce the optimally good world in accord with human freedom. He will save as many as He can—*all* those who desire to do His will freely (John 6:37; 7:17). The fact that some men refuse to be saved does not veto the right of others to go God's way nor does it veto the right of God to make a world in which all may choose the way they will go. God is not morally responsible if some refuse to eat; He has graciously provided the Bread of Life for all (John 6:35). From God's standpoint, too, it is better to have loved and lost than never to have loved at all. It is better to have created creatures and to have given them the offer of eternal life—knowing some would refuse it—than not to offer it at all.* As C. S. Lewis observed in a similar connection, it is morally wrong to demand that unless all "consent to be happy (on their own terms) no one else shall taste joy . . . that Hell should be able to *veto* Heaven."[42]

In conclusion, we have seen that there are coherent theistic solutions to the problem of moral evil. Of all

---

*For a discussion concerning those who have never heard the gospel and objections to theism concerning hell, see appendices 1 and 2.

the worlds that could be created, this world is the best possible way to obtain the best possible world, i.e., one where the greatest number of persons are given the maximal eternal joy and where the freedom of all creatures is respected. Further, we have seen that the moral objections raised against this theistic system to have reasonable answers. In the next chapter, we will investigate the theistic solutions to the problem of physical evil.

Explanations for Physical Evil

Chapter Abstract

Biblical theism is applied to the physical problems of evil.

chapter six

Explanations for Physical Evil

The solutions to the problems of metaphysical and moral evil do not, in and of themselves, solve the problem of physical evil. The solution to the problem of metaphysical evil (i.e., evil is a privation) merely shows how evil is possible in a perfectly good, finite world created by an absolutely perfect God. The answer to the problem of moral evil merely shows how good creatures could activate evil by freely choosing their own finite preferences above the infinite good of God.

But neither of these indicates why there are many *physical* evils in the world that do not appear to be the result of any free choices. For instance, why do many innocent people suffer from floods, earthquakes, and tornadoes? There seems to be no connection with their own free choices nor any justification for their innocent suffering. If nature were an independent entity operating autonomously apart from God, the theist might have ready recourse to an answer. But the problem is 67 made more acute for a theist since he believes God is in sovereign control of the natural world.

One of the most famous contemporary examples of an objection to theism from the point of physical evil can be seen in the example used previously from the *The Plague* by Albert Camus.[43] The logic may be summarized as follows:

> Either one must join the doctor and fight the plague God sent for man's sin, or else he must join the priest and not fight the plague.
> But not to fight the plague is inhumane.
> And to fight the plague is to fight against God who sent it.
> Hence, if humanitarianism is right, then theism is wrong.
> Humanitarianism is right, and it is right to work to alleviate suffering.
> Therefore, theism is wrong.

There are several assumptions the theist would challenge in Camus's argument. First, according to the Bible, one cannot conclude that people who suffer tragedy through natural disaster are suffering because they are more wicked than those who are not likewise suffering (see Luke 13:3, 4). Second, if the "plague" is viewed broadly as the curse of sin on the whole fallen world, then it might be better to describe it as what man brought on himself by his own free choice (Gen. 3:14; 5:12; 8:19, 20). Third, it is not wrong for a theist to work against unjust suffering. In fact, because it was man who brought the fall to the world (brought evil into the world), he can work to remove the effects of that fall (i.e., suffering) without being concerned about fighting against God. Fourth, although the biblical theist is concerned for the plague's victims, he works against the general plague of evil at the most effective level—the *cause* of the plague, not merely the *results*. Evil is the ultimate cause of plague, even physical evils, and the life-transforming message of the cross of Jesus Christ is the most effective cure for evil known to man. It is not wrong—in fact, it is good—to treat symptoms and put bandages on suffering men, but it is even better to treat and cure the disease that is causing the sickness. Christian theism offers exactly what is needed—an internal change in man that enables him to overcome evil.

The objection has been raised by H. J. McCloskey[44] that the theist is morally obligated not to work against suffering because:

> The theist is morally obligated to promote the greatest good.
> But according to theism, the greatest good cannot be achieved if suffering is eliminated.
> Hence, the theist is morally obligated to promote suffering.

The theist may respond to this argument by pointing out that certain evils are only to be *permitted* but not to be actively promoted. The theist is not obligated to promote evil means in order to attain good ends. Hence, he is not, by duty, bound to promote suffering to attain greater goods. For example, a parent may *permit* his child the pain of the dentist's drill in order to promote the pleasure of better teeth. The biblical theist is, in fact, admonished to *promote good* in the world and to relieve the suffering of those who are afflicted (Luke 10:30-37).

Furthermore, if the theist works to eliminate suffering, he will not destroy the possibility of a great good being achieved by the preconditioning presence of evil. God knows that men will not be able to abolish evil and that there will be enough suffering to occasion the greater good. God does not have to promote or produce the suffering, since it is already present in sufficient quantities to achieve the greater good.

The most pressing objection to theism in the area of physical evil is the existence of unjustified suffering in the world. The argument can be formulated in this way:

> There are many occurrences of unjustified suffering in the world.

But even one instance of unjustified suffering shows
there is no perfectly just God.
Therefore, there is no God.

The strength of this argument is based on two points:
the obvious fact that not all suffering is self-inflicted or
deserved and the fact that only one instance of unjustified suffering would disprove the God of theism.
Who could argue that the suffering of every cancer
victim, every earthquake casualty, or every child or-
phaned by disease was justified? Thus it would appear
that God has allowed an injustice, and, therefore does
not exist or, if He does, is not really just.

Before some possible justifications are presented for
all physical evil in the world, it is important to repeat
two points. First, the attempt will not be made to
account for all allegedly *innocent* suffering. Surely
many personally innocent people suffer. The question
is not whether they were innocent (admittedly, they
may have been personally blameless) but whether their
innocent suffering is *justifiable*. Second, not all immediately unjustified suffering will be *ultimately* unjustified. The wrongs of today may be righted tomor-
row, and the injustices of this life may be justified in
the next life. This thesis is both possible and verifiable
in the future.

It is incumbent upon the theist, however, to present
some plausible explanation for the *apparently* unjustified suffering that occurs in this world. Critics of this
view would say that this is not the best of all possible
worlds; but, if it is, as was argued in the previous
chapters, the best of all possible *ways* to the best
world, then how can it contain so many apparent injustices?

The burden of a theistic theodicy, then, is to show
how one hundred percent of the suffering in this world
can be justified.* And since the heart of the theistic
theodicy is that evil emanates from free will and that
this evil world is the best way to the best world, *it must
be possible to show how all suffering is connected with
free will and is necessary for the opportunity and
attainment of the greatest good achievable*. In short,

all physical evil must be necessary to the moral purposes of God in granting free choice and in producing the greatest good. In view of these directives, let us examine several reasons for physical evil that, when taken together, seem to explain one hundred percent of the evil in the world.

1. *Some physical evil comes to us directly from our own free choices.* It is good to be free, and freedom is an essential part of a moral world. A puppet creation is not a moral one. But if one is free, then he is free to bring certain evils on himself. Abuse of one's body, for example, will bring sickness. Overeating will bring obesity, and underexercise may result in heart problems. Excessive smoking may contribute to lung cancer. It is said that when one man read in his newspaper that conclusive evidence had linked smoking with lung cancer, he canceled his subscription. These are all part of the evils one may directly bring on himslef by his own free choices. These and many other forms of suffering are part of the possible pains that accompany the privilege of being free.

Ten Reasons for Physical Evil

2. *Some physical evils come to us indirectly from the exercise of our freedom.* Suffering might come from choosing to do nothing. Free creatures have the option of being lazy. But poverty often results from laziness and so, in this way, the pain of being poor may be indirectly caused by one's own free choice to remain idle. The same is true of numerous other problems we face in later life because of the choice not to plan ahead properly. Even cultivating bad habits, such as driving while tired, may involve free choices that may cause later suffering.

3. *Some physical evils come to us directly from the free choices of others.* It is often true that we suffer at the hands of other free creatures (and they at our

---

*It is important to note that the atheist does not succeed by default if the theist fails to explain all evils. It is always possible that God has a good purpose for allowing suffering—a purpose that is not known to the theist (see Deut. 29:29; Rom. 11:33).

hands). In a free world, child abuse is possible, as is wife-beating and mugging. In a physical world of more than one free being, conflict is possible. Given the nature of free choice and a significant number of persons, one might suspect that conflict and pain were inevitable. In these cases, there is certainly innocent suffering and even immediately unjustified pain. However, this is all a part of the price we pay as free creatures to exercise our choices in individual autonomy.

4. *Some physical evil comes to us indirectly from the free choices of others.* Improper prenatal care has caused many sicknesses and handicaps for children. Likwise, parental laziness can cause child poverty. Even more remotely, ancestral choices (of occupation, location, or political affiliation) have long-range consequences on generations to come. In fact, it might be said that *all* of the rest of physical evils both in man and nature are connected with our ancestors' freedom of choice. These first four reasons alone may account for one hundred percent of the physical evil and suffering in a free moral world.[45] Despite this possibility, more can be said of other possible sources of physical evil.

5. *Some physical evil may be a necessary by-product of other good activities.*[46] In a physical world where there is water for boating and swimming, some will drown. If there are mountains to climb, there must also be valleys into which one may fall. If there are cars to drive, collisions can also occur.

It may be said that tornadoes, lightning, hurricanes, and other natural disasters are likewise by-products of a good physical world. For instance, the *purpose* of rain is not to flood or drown, but the result of rain may include these disasters. Likewise, hot and cold air are an essential and purposeful part of the physical world, but under certain conditions they may combine to form tornadoes.

6. *Some evils may come upon us as the result of the choices of evil spirits.*[47] In a world that widely believes in beings on other planets, as well as various kinds of spiritual phenomena, it is not difficult for many to believe there are spirits who visit this planet. Accord-

ing to the Bible, there are evil spirits who not only visit

this earth but have also been known to inflict physical evil on men who live here (Mark 9:20, Luke 13:10-16). Job's sufferings are so attributed to Satan (Job 1:6, 7). Also there were people in Jesus' day who were said to be oppressed and afflicted with diseases from the devil (Matt. 17:14-15).

7. *Some physical evils are God-given warnings of greater physical evils.* Not all pain is bad. Warning pains, like alarm systems, are good since they help prevent greater ills. Toothaches can help prevent future tooth decay, and chest pains, if heeded, may prevent needless death. Hunger pains can lead not only to the avoidance of pain but also the pleasurable experience of eating and the resulting stability of health. In these senses, some physical pains are not unjust but are highly justified.

8. *Some physical suffering may be used by God as a warning about moral evils.* God may use (or even sometimes send) physical pain as a moral warning. Many men have testified to the purifying and perfecting work of pain in their lives. Job suffered much and said, "When he has tried me, I shall come forth as gold" (Job 23:10). C. S. Lewis hit the nail on the head when he wrote, "God whispers to us in our pleasures, speaks in our conscience, but shouts in our pains: it is His megaphone to rouse a deaf world."[48] This is no argument for stoicism or sadism. However, much of the physical pain of the world can be a very effective means of alerting men to danger, thereby promoting the avoidance of moral evil and the attainment of vastly higher moral good.

9. *Some physical evil may be permitted as a condition of greater moral perfection.* There is undoubtedly an overlap here with many of the functions of pain already stated. That is, where finite free choice is the cause of the evil, God may still use it as an instrument of moral perfection. Without tribulation there would be no virtue of patience, and without sin there would be no enjoyment of forgiveness. Of course, we do not promote sin as the only means to virtue. Nevertheless, God is able to overrule man's intentions and use our

evil to fulfill His own good purposes. As Paul wrote, "We know that in all things God works for the good of those who love him" (Rom. 8:28). Even when men intend evil by their acts, God can accomplish good through those acts. Joseph's brothers sold him as a slave. But later when he was able to punish his brothers, he forgivingly rescued them saying, "You intended to harm me; but God intended it for good" (Gen. 50:20).

10. *Finally, some physical evil occurs because higher forms live on lower ones.* In this kind of world, the early bird gets the worm and eats it. While that might be good for the bird, it isn't so good for the worm! Plants and animals die so that man may live. One life form is sacrificed for another life form in order to provide food energy for the survival of the higher form. Since we live in a physical world governed by physical laws of energy flow, it is possible that this is the only way a physical world could be constructed.

In conclusion, we can say that much of the physical evil in the world is a result of the free choices of autonomous creatures on this earth. Evil can be justified as the way to the best possible world: it is essential to the testing and perfection of morally free and redeemable creatures who alone make it possible for the achievement of the best possible world.

A Final Objection Answered

One final objection to the above solutions to the problems of physical evil demands attention. Why doesn't God miraculously intervene and prevent all physical evil from occuring, but permit all physical good to remain? For example, why doesn't God intercept the murderer's bullets but not the hunter's? Why not turn the assassin's knife to jelly but not the butcher's? Why not transform the rioter's rocks to cotton and the strangler's noose to a noodle?

There is no question that God has the power to do so. An omnipotent Creator is in sovereign control of His creation and has the ability to perform miraculous events. Anyone who can make something from nothing has no trouble turning water into wine or effecting any other such transformation. If God does not lack the power, then He must lack the will. But why? There are some very good reasons.

First, evil men do not really want God to intercept *every* evil act or thought. No one wants to get a headache every time he thinks against God. One does not want God to fill his mouth with cotton when he speaks evil of God, nor does he really desire God to explode his pen as he writes against God or destroy his books before they come off the press. At best, people really want God to intercept only *some* evil actions. But theists may argue that God is doing precisely that. He is intercepting *some* evil actions by the influences for good He has placed in the world (such as the Holy Spirit, the Bible, Christians, and the moral law). Only rarely does He need to intercede through miraculous action.

Second, continual interference would disrupt the regularity of natural law and make life impossible. Everyday living depends on physical laws such as inertia or gravity. Regular interruption of these would make everyday life impossible and a human being extremely edgy! Third, it is probable that chaos would result from continued miraculous intervention. Imagine children throwing knives at parents because they know they will be turned to rubber, and parents driving cars through stop signs, knowing God will create crash-protection air shields to avert any ensuing collisions. The necessary intervention would finally grow in proportions that would effectively remove human freedom and responsibility. Not only so but undoubtedly God would be frequently caught in dilemmas. The sadist would be thwarted in his self-actualization, if every time he intended to torture or kill someone, God intervened. Which evil does God then choose?*

---

*It is of note that such a dilemma of intervention exists in biblical theism. Here we see the belief that God allowed Jesus to suffer and die on the cross in order to save man. One of the soldiers even calls upon Jesus to perform a miracle and save himself (Luke 23:37). In this case, performing a miracle to save Jesus from the cross would have prevented man's salvation.

If human freedom and responsiblity were removed, then there would be two major difficulties in this hypothetical world that happily we do not have to experience in the best of all ways to the best possible world. First, if God were to prevent all evil acts from occurring, He would have to interfere with the full exercise of free choice—leaving us with a world something less than fully moral, if it could be considered to be moral at all. Second, in a world of constant divine intervention of evil actions, all moral learning would cease. Men would never learn by the evil consequences of bad choices. If all evil actions were stopped, then men would not learn the consequences of evil thoughts or actions. And if all moral learning ceased, then redeemability and perfectability would also vanish. Who would want to live in a world where there is not potential for moral progress or achievement?

In summation, it should be noted that all physical evil is either a consequence, a condition, or a concomitant of free choice. Further, physical evil is not desired by God but is used by Him, nonetheless, to occasion the full exercise of free choice and to maximize the opportunity for attaining the greatest good achievable in a fully free, moral world.

Concluding
Remarks
About Evil

Chapter Abstract

Some concluding remarks are made about the existence of evil and its place in the ultimate plan of God in the universe.

chapter seven

Concluding Remarks About Evil

The problem of evil is a difficult philosophical question. The sheer number of philosophic options regarding evil testifies to man's continuing quest to create a philosophic system that answers the major questions posed by the existence of evil. Illusionism seeks to bring resolve by denying the reality of evil. Dualism seeks to answer the question by positing an eternal existence of both good and evil. Finitism, sadism, and impossiblism seek explanations by altering our notions of God's attributes or abilities. And atheism denies the dilemma itself by denying the existence of God.

It seems evident from the foregoing study that the one philosophic system that *does* provide the most satisfactory answers is the greatest-way theodicy, and in particular, biblical theism. It is of even greater note that as man comes to know more about the true nature of reality, he discovers that the view of reality portrayed in biblical theism is remarkably similar to the

79

nature of reality as observed. This is curious simply because biblical theism claims to be more than simply a philosophic system devised by an ancient Hebrew people. It claims to be revelation from an intelligent, personal, all-knowing, all-loving, all-powerful God. Its similarity to reality is not surprising, since the historic Christian position holds this reality to be the result of the Creator.

The historic Christian position states that man was created in the image of God and was placed on earth with the power of free choice. Man through his willful free choice brought evil into the world. Our moral nature is a testimony to the reality of a moral structure within the universe, and our cruelty is a testimony to the sinful nature within man. It also explains the basic frustration, loneliness, and alienation felt by man, who is cut off from a higher reality since he is no longer in a normal state. Man can work against evil in the world without fear that he is working against God, since evil in the world is a result of man's free choice, and it is present only by God's permission as the way to the best of all possible worlds.

As we noted in the section on atheism, it is impossible to deny God without implying that God exists. In order to complain about unjustified suffering, one must suppose an ultimate moral standard within the universe. As we have shown, these arguments have a boomerang effect that actually supports the claims of biblical theism. In fact, it is impossible to sustain philosophically any human values at all from the position of atheism.

We are right to ask about the existence of God and we are right to ask the moral question. The Christian position does provide answers to these questions because we do live in a world created by a moral, loving, and powerful God. This, in fact, is the optimism of Christianity. Since there is an all-powerful God who *can* defeat evil without destroying free choice, and since there is an all-loving God who *wants* to defeat evil without destroying free choice, then there is the assured hope that He *will* destroy evil in the future. The ultimate optimism of Christianity is that in the future there will be a time when evil is rendered null and void.

But Christianity holds more than just the ultimate hope of the eventual destruction of evil. It provides immediate satisfaction and power to deal with the sinful nature of man. The historic Christian position is that God *desires* to restore man to a vital personal relationship with Himself through man's faith in God through the death of Jesus Christ for man's sin. The debt of sin and evil has been paid and man has only to receive it.

What About Those Who Have Not Heard?

A discussion about heaven and hell often leads to another question that should be answered: What happens to those who have not heard anything about God and the way they might be saved? To gain a complete answer to this question is impossible, since even in biblical theism this has not been totally revealed. There are, however, certain principles that may be applied to gain a perspective on this question.

First, it should be noted that from the perspective of biblical theism, God never intended hell for man. God is holy and loving and wishes that every person would come to repentance (Exod. 34:6, 7; Jonah 4:10, 11; 2 Peter 3:9). Though the God of biblical theism is a God of justice and righteousness, He is also portrayed as a God of love.

Second, the very nature of God prevents Him from being unfair. He will do right in His judgment and execute it with equity (Gen. 18:25; Ps. 7:11; 9:18; 1 Peter 1:17). He is very different from a judge we might

83

go before in an earthly court, since His very character causes Him to be fair to those before Him.

Third, we see from biblical theism the claim that men are *not* in total spiritual darkness. There are numerous verses that state that man has an awareness of God and an awareness of eternity (Ps. 19:1-4; Eccles. 3:11; John 1:9; Acts 14:15-17; Rom. 1:18-21; 2:15). It was Seneca, the Roman sage, who said, "God is near you, is with you. A sacred Spirit dwells within us, the Observer and Guardian of all our evil and all our good. There is no good man without God."[49] The universal human sense of morality, in fact, would seem to imply an ultimate moral standard beyond man.

Fourth, biblical theism is very clear in its statement that anyone who wishes to establish a relationship with God will receive the necessary information on which to make a decision. God is described as the rewarder of those who seek Him (Heb. 11:6), and the claim is repeatedly made that God gives the essential guidance required to lead a person to Himself (1 Chron. 28:9; 2 Chron. 15:2; Pss. 9:10; 146:17-20; Prov. 8:17; Jer. 29:13; Acts 8:30, 31).

Fifth, the responsibility for a decision concerning salvation is in the hands of each person. Each of us is ultimately responsible for the course he chooses. In this context, C. W. Hale Amos wrote, "From what we do know, respecting the terms of our own salvation, we are led irresistibly to the conclusion that no man can perish except by his own fault and deliberate choice."[50]

In conclusion, we should recognize that although we do not have a total answer to this question from the perspective of biblical theism, we do have some principles that can be used. These indicate that God is willing that all come to repentance and that He is a fair judge. They also indicate that man is not in total spiritual darkness and that the ultimate decision concerning his destiny is his own.

Objections to Theism Concerning Evil

The question of hell is certainly a difficult one; but it would be dishonest to say that the New Testament does not speak of a place called hell. Because it does, there are a number of objections that have been raised. They deserve answers.

The first objection that is often raised is whether it isn't intolerable that eternal punishment be given for temporal sins. In other words, why should someone be punished eternally for an action that occurred at a moment in time? Isn't this a serious case of overkill? The answer to this is that it certainly would be overkill if people were forced to go to hell against their will.

God consigns men to their destinies only in accordance with their choices. We should be clear that an all-knowing God is not limited in knowledge simply to the day-by-day good and bad things men do, nor is an all-loving God going to condemn men for these "small" things. It is, rather, that in response to the gospel, either overtly or ultimately, somewhere in the midst of a life of these small choices, each person makes the larger decision of his ultimate allegiance. It may be said that a lifetime is long enough to make a lifetime decision. There is much biblical stress placed on the significance of decisions made in this life (Heb. 2:3).

Hell can be defined as that place where men are separated from God. The real "hell" of hell seems to be the complete privation of God and all goodness, in the face of clear knowledge of these blessings (Luke 13:28; 16:23). Just as metaphysical evil is a privation of good, and could not be known without good, so the distress of hell is at least partially in knowing what one is missing. Thus the torment of the rich man in hell described in the Gospel of Luke is made even worse because he can see across a great chasm to what his life might have been (Luke 16:26).

Man may not *want* to be in hell, but neither does man *will* the condition of his release. An omniscient God knows that man will never change his mind; otherwise, He would never have let him go there in the first place. The choice is permanent and irreversible. The reckless driver who "totals" his car may not wish it to be wrecked, but he has willed the permanent condition. So it is with man's life. A man can "total" his soul.

A second objection is whether it would be better for God to annihilate men rather than to allow them to suffer consciously forever. First of all, we must acknowlege that it would not be true justice if God were to simply snuff out of existence men who did not go His way. That would make God no different from any of hundreds of earthly dictators who have lived. Second, if God had given Nietzsche the choice to: (1) renounce his atheism, (2) be swept into nonexistence, or (3) go on willing the eternal recurrence of the same meaningless state of affairs forever (a possible description of hell), Nietzsche made it clear that he would have chosen conscious suffering apart from God. "Man," he wrote, "needs a goal—and he would rather will nothingness than not will at all."[51] When faced with the real choices of submitting to God, losing one's freedom by annihilation, or retaining one's free choice to reject God, many would agree with the Satan of Milton's *Paradise Lost:*

> We shall be free; th' Almighty hath not built
> Here for his envy will not drive us hence:
> Here we may reign secure, and in my choice
> To reign is worthy ambition though in hell:
> Better to reign in hell than to serve in heaven.[52]

A third objection is often raised about the possible happiness one could have in heaven knowing that a loved one is suffering in hell. This question is based on the assumption that men are more merciful than God. But if the happiness of the good were dependent upon the will of the wicked, then those evil forces could "blackmail the universe." No unselfish person should feel guilty for enjoying his lunch simply because there are starving people in the world. This would be particularly true if he had offered to share his goods with the others, but they had refused to eat.

A fourth objection that might be raised is why God would create men whom He knew would reject Him and go to hell. For one thing, even those who reject God are part of this best possible way to the best possible world. It is better to offer good even knowing that some will reject it, than not to offer it at all. There is always a risk in love—the risk that it will be rejected. God took that "risk," since it was better to create a world where the greatest good possible *could* be attained by all, even though some would willfully reject it. In doing so, the net result is the greatest good *achievable* by all in a free universe.

A fifth objection, How can it be said that evil is defeated if so many people lose and go to Hell? There are several ways in which sin is defeated in this kind of universe. Good triumphs over evil in the lives of all who have reached heaven; evil is permitted and defeated under various conditions; and evil is defeated by being separated and quarantined from the rest of the universe. Weeds and wheat grow together until the harvest, but they must eventually be separated if there is to be good bread. In the same way, good and evil will increase together, but there will be a final separation of the good from the evil. Good will survive and flourish, but evil will "die" and be "destroyed forever."

Sixth, one might object, "If hell is what some prefer, then hell must be desirable." The answer to this is that hell is not what men *want* (desire), but it is what they *will* (decide to do). Men do not *want* war, but neither do they *will* to eliminate what causes it. Unless we begin to will conditions of peace, we will continue to have war. A wino doesn't *want* a hangover, but he *wills* himself one when he drinks. So it is with hell. Those who go there choose the conditions but do not relish the consequences. It is, after all, described as a place of "weeping and grinding of teeth" (Matt. 8:12).

This might lead to a seventh and last objection, What if someone changes his mind after he gets to hell? God, in His infinite knowledge, knows that more opportunities would not help. If one or two more days, or even years, would have brought a person to God, surely He would have granted it. "The Lord is . . . patient . . . , not wanting anyone to perish, but everyone to come to repentance" (2 Peter 3:9). Although Jesus made the statement that Sodom and Gomorrah would have repented if they had seen the miracles that he performed (Matt. 11:20-24), this should be understood as a hypothetical hyperbole to indicate the severity of the listeners' sin. This is indicated by both the parallel passage, which used the phrase "it will be more bearable" (Matt. 11:24) for them in the day of judgment, and the fact that Jesus said elsewhere, "They will not be convinced even if someone rises from the dead" (Luke 16:31). God knows how many chances a person needs before he has made his final decision, and He knows when no amount of additional opportunities will change that decision.

Response

JOHN W.
WENHAM

Evil constitutes the biggest single argument against the existence of an almighty, loving God. At the same time its study provides the most direct route to an understanding of the way the universe is run. The subject is crucial to those who are searching for truth and wishing to grapple with the claims of Christianity, and to Christians who wish to deepen their grasp and come to grips with their doubts. It is good to have Dr. Geisler's lucid and thoughtful introduction to this tremendous topic, which he has brought well within the reach of the educated reader who has no special knowledge of theology or philosophy.

In an attempted "justifying of the ways of God to man" it is important to remember that God is God and man is man, and that none of us can get our finite minds around the greatness of the divine being. When we have done our utmost thinking, God's thoughts are still higher than our thoughts. Nevertheless, not to think at all is an even greater folly than to think imperfectly.

One of the useful ways of thinking is to examine the various alternatives to Christian theism. Many feel the force of objections to Christianity without realizing that alternative philosophies are open to even greater objections. Dr. Geisler points out their weaknesses one by one. In the process of doing this he clarified, by contrast, the positions of the biblical faith. His exposition of the thought of Augustine of Hippo, who asserted the reality of evil but denied to it the status of a "thing," is particularly valuable. He shows that all evil derives from the will of free agents who refuse good. Evil is not something created by God; it is the result of losses sustained through wrong choices. Also most valuable is the author's contrast of the two concepts "this is the best of all possible worlds" and "this is the *best way* to the best of all possible worlds." The beginner especially will find the book a veritable mine of insight through valid arguments. It will drive many readers, whether by whetting their appetites or even by

89

evoking strong disagreement, to further study of the Bible itself. For *nowhere* is the reality of evil more vividly and ruthlessly displayed than in the Scriptures of the Old and New Testament. And *nowhere* is its ultimate defeat more clearly set out. At the heart of the story stands the cross of Christ, where evil did its worst and met its match. It is there that the roots of evil are fully revealed and it is there that the almighty God of love shines forth.

References

[1]See Parmenides, "The Proem," in G. S. Kirk and J. E. Raven, *The Presocratic Philosophers* (Cambridge: Cambridge University Press, 1964), pp. 266-67.

[2]Mary Baker Eddy, *Science and Health with Key to the Scriptures* (Boston: Christian Science Publishing, 1906), pp. 113, 289, 480.

[3]M. Hiriyanna, *The Essentials of Indian Philosophy* (London: George Allen and Unwin, 1949), pp. 153-54.

[4]See St. Augustine's account of the Manichaean teaching in his anti-Manichaean writings in Philip Schaff, ed., *The Nicene and Post-Nicene Fathers* (Grand Rapids: Eerdmans, 1956).

[5]Thomas Aquinas, *Basic Writings of Saint Thomas Aquinas,* ed. Anton C. Pegis, Vol. 1: *Summa Theologica,* I, 48, 3 (New York: Random, 1945).

[6]See especially Part V in Alfred North Whitehead, *Process and Reality* (New York: Harper and Row, 1929).

[7]Ibid., pp. 352, 523-33.

[8]Adapted from E. H. Madden and P. H. Hare, *Evil and the Concept of God* (Springfield, Ill.: Charles C. Thomas, 1968). See especially chapter 6.

[9]Ibid.

[10]See chapters 16 and 17 in Edward J. Carnell, *An Introduction to Christian Apologetics* (Grand Rapids: Eerdmans, 1950).

[11]William James, *The Varieties of Religious Experience* (New York: The New American Library of World Literature, 1958), p. 55.

[12]Rene Descartes, *Meditations I,* trans. L. Lafleur (New York: Bobbs-Merrill, Liberal Arts, 1951).

[13]Charles Hartshorne, "The Necessary Existent," in *The Ontological Argument,* ed. Alvin Plantinga (New York: Doubleday, 1965), p. 127.

[14]See discussion in chapter 4 of Nelson Pike, *God and Timelessness* (New York: Shocken, 1970).

[15]Aquinas, *Summa Theologica,* I, 10, 2 and I, 14, 13.

[16]Bertrand Russell, "Why I am not a Christian," in *The*

91

Basic Writings of Bertrand Russell (New York: Simon and Schuster, 1961), pp. 585-86.

[17] E. Beller and M. Lee, eds., *Selections from Bayle's Dictionary* (Princeton, N. J.: Princeton University Press, 1952), pp. 157-83.

[18] John Hicks has argued that a position is at least meaningful to hold if one can specify the conditions in the future under which it can be verified. John Hick, "Theology and Verification," *The Existence of God* (New York: Macmillan, 1964), pp. 253-54.

[19] H. J. McCloskey, "God and Evil," in *The Philosophical Quarterly* (April 1960), reprinted in Nelson Pike, *God and Evil* (New York: Prentice Hall, 1964).

[20] C. S. Lewis, *Mere Christianity* (New York: Macmillan, 1960), pp. 45-46.

[21] See my discussion in *Philosophy of Religion* (Grand Rapids: Zondervan, 1974), pp. 349-50.

[22] Augustine, *On order,* I, 1, 2; III, vii, 49; II, iv, in Schaff, *Fathers.*

[23] Idem, *On the Nature of the Good,* XXXVIII in Schaff, *Fathers.*

[24] Gottfried Leibniz, *Theodicy,* trans. E. M. Huggard (Indianapolis: Bobbs-Merrill, 1966).

[25] For an excellent study of verses misused to support theistic determinism, see parts 2 and 3 in Roger T. Forest and V. Paul Marston, *God's Strategy in Human History* (Wheaton, Ill.: Tyndale, 1974).

[26] Augustine, *Nature of Good.*

[27] Ibid., XVII.

[28] Idem, *On the Morals of the Manichaeans,* IX, 14, in Schaff, *Fathers.*

[29] Idem, *Nature of Good,* XXVII.

[30] Idem, *Against the Epistle of the Manichaeans,* XXXVIII, 44, in Schaff, *Fathers.*

[31] Augustine, *On Free Will,* I, 1, 1; III, xvii, 76; in Schaff, *Fathers.*

[32] Ibid., III, XXV, 76.

[33] Plotinus, *Enneads,* I, 7, 1, trans. Stephen MacKenna (London: Faber and Faber, 1966).

[34] Benedict Spinoza, *The Ethics,* Part I, Proposition XVI, in

The Rationalists (New York: Doubleday, 1960), Part I, Appendix.

[35]C. S. Lewis makes an unnecessary concession by suggesting that God could not have created other possible worlds in *The Problem of Pain* (New York: Macmillan, 1962), p. 35.

[36]Douglas Gilbert and Clyde Kilby, *C. S. Lewis: Images of His World,* (Grand Rapids: Eerdmans, 1973), p. 21.

[37]Peter Koestenbaum, "Religion in the Tradition of Phenomenology," in *Religion in Philosophical and Cultural Perspective,* ed., J. Clayton Feaver and William Horosz (Princeton, N. J.: Van Nostrand, 1967), p. 212.

[38]John Hick, *Evil and the God of Love* (New York: Harper and Row, 1966), pp. 374f.

[39]Walter Kauffmann, *Critique of Religion and Philosophy* (New York: Anchor Books, 1961), p. 135.

[40]C. S. Lewis, *The Great Divorce* (New York: Macmillan, 1946), p. 69.

[41]Idem, *Four Loves* (New York: Harcourt Brace Javanovich, 1960), p. 18.

[42]C. S. Lewis, *Great Divorce,* pp. 110-11.

[43]Albert Camus, *The Plague,* trans. S. Gilbert (New York: Alfred A. Knopf, 1948).

[44]H. J. McClosky, "God and Evil," *The Philosophical Quarterly* (April 1960).

[45]C. S. Lewis estimated that 4/5 of all evil comes from persons being nasty to each other *(The Problem of Pain,* p. 86). Hugh Silvester believes the percentage should be closer to 19/20. See his *Arguing with God* (Downers Grove, Ill.: Inter-Varsity, 1972), p.32.

[46]F. R. Tennant, *Philosophical Theology* (Cambridge: Cambridge University Press, 1930), Volume II.

[47]Alvin Plantinga, "Free Will Defense," in *God and Other Minds* (Ithaca, N. Y.: Cornell University Press, 1970).

[48]Lewis, *Problem of Pain,* p. 93.

[49]J. Oswald Saunders, *How Lost Are the Heathen?* (Chicago: Moody, 1972), p. 53.

[50]Ibid., p. 54.

[51]Friedrich Nietzsche, *The Genealogy of Morals* (New York: Random, Vintage 1969), sec. 28, p. 163.

[52]John Milton, *Paradise Lost,* I, 259-263.

For Further Reading

Augustinus, Aurelius (Saint Augustine). "The Nature of the Good" in the Library of Christian Classics. Philadelphia: Westminster, 1953. Vol. 6: **Augustine: Earlier Writings.** Selected and translated by John H. S. Burleigh.

The classic Christian refutation to the dualistic solution to evil. Augustine stresses that evil is by nature a privation of good and by source it springs from the misuse of free will.

See also by Saint Augustine, **On Order,** 1, 1, s. in Philip Schaff, ed. **The Nicene and Post-Nicene Fathers.** Grand Rapids: Eerdmans, 1956.

Carnell, E. J. **Introduction to Christian Apologetics.** Grand Rapids: Eerdmans, 1948.

This work, written primarily for Christians, contains a response to the finite-godism answer to evil. The author stresses the inadequacy of such a system by showing that a finite god cannot guarantee evil will be overthrown, nor can the believer be properly motivated to fight evil in view of this god's impotence.

Farrer, Austin. **Love Almighty and Ills Unlimited.** Garden City: Doubleday, 1961; also, London: Collins, 1962.

As a Neothomist (one seeking to restore the Catholic philosophy of Aquinas to fit the present age), this well-known contemporary theologian utilizes some elements of Neoplatonism and modern science to explain the presence of certain evils in the world.

Leibniz, Gottfried. **Theodicy.** Translated by E. M. Huggard. London: Routledge and Kegan Paul, 1951.

Leibniz has been considered the foremost spokesman of optimism and rationalism. His view of evil as an instrument to work for cosmic good is known as the best-of-all-possible-worlds solution.

Lewis, C. S. **The Problem of Pain.** New York: Macmillan, 1961.

This famous literary lay theologian emphasizes the value of pain as God's "'megaphone" to arouse a morally insensitive world where evil is a reality.

Lewis, C. S. **A Grief Observed.** New York: Bantam, 1976.

A subjective response to evil in the death of his wife. A good companion reader to his more objective, and earlier, treatment in The Problem of Pain.

Lewis, C. S. **The Great Divorce.** New York: Macmillan, 1946.

An interesting and speculative, though worthwhile, treatment of the nature of evil and the interplay between human choice and evil.

Plantinga, Alvin. **God, Freedom, and Evil.** New York: Harper and Row, 1974.

A reputable contemporary Christian philosopher states the free-will defense for the analytic philosopher.

Ramm, Bernard L. **The God Who Makes a Difference.** Waco, Texas: Word, 1972.

Chapter 8, 9, and 10 deal with the problem of evil and the Christian faith, surveying the literature and evaluating the arguments as well as some of the biblical texts.

Silvester, Hugh. **Arguing with God.** Downers Grove: InterVarsity, 1971.

Silvester has written a good general-purpose reader for a Christian examination of evil. It is aimed primarily at Christians, but would be useful for interested unbelievers also.

Tennant, F. R. **Philosophical Theology.** 2 volumes. Cambridge: Cambridge University Press, 1937.

This highly technical and theological work will be of interest to the philosophy student with particular concern in natural theology. Tennant views evil as an inherent consequence of man's existence in the world as it is.

Thomas Aquinas, Saint. **Basic Writings of Saint Thomas Aquinas.** Edited by Anton C. Pegis. Vol. 2: **Summa Contra Gentiles,** III, 1-22. New York: Random, 1945.

Aquinas is known for his synthesis of philosophy and faith. His work is the accepted basis for most modern Roman Catholic theology. He provides a further development and systematization of Augustine's thoughts on evil.

Wenham, John William. **The Goodness of God.** Downers Grove: InterVarsity, 1975.

A very helpful treatment for those who are interested in dealing with the problem of evil and God's goodness in reality more than theory. Wenham seriously entertains the possibility of the annihilation of the wicked, an untraditional view of hell.